Mardi Gras

CHRONICLES OF THE NEW ORLEANS CARNIVAL

A masker at a New Orleans society ball. (Photo by Peggy Scott Laborde)

Mardi Gras

CHRONICLES OF THE NEW ORLEANS CARNIVAL

BY ERROL LABORDE

WITH PRINCIPAL PHOTOGRAPHY BY MITCHEL L. OSBORNE

FOREWORD BY PEGGY SCOTT LABORDE

PELICAN PUBLISHING COMPANY

GRETNA 2013

*The word "Pelican" and the depiction of a pelican are
trademarks of Pelican Publishing Company, Inc., and are
registered in the U.S. Patent and Trademark Office.*

Library of Congress Cataloging-in-Publication Data

Laborde, Errol, 1947-
  Mardi Gras : chronicles of the New Orleans carnival / Errol Laborde ; with principal
photography by Mitchel L. Osborne ; foreword by Peggy Scott Laborde.
       pages cm.
  Includes index.
  ISBN 978-1-4556-1764-7 (hc : alk. paper) — ISBN 978-1-4556-1765-4 (e-book)
1. Carnival—Louisiana—New Orleans—History. 2. New Orleans (La.)—Social life
and customs. I. Title.
  GT4211.N4L33 2013
  394.2509763'35--dc23
                                    2013017226

Printed in Singapore
Published by Pelican Publishing Company, Inc.
1000 Burmaster Street, Gretna, Louisiana 70053

Marching Order

A flambeau carrier in the Orpheus parade. (Photo © Mitchel Osborne)

Foreword

Some well-meaning folks have assumed that my husband, Errol, and I live and breathe Mardi Gras. After all, our home has rooms painted purple (closer to eggplant), green, and gold (maybe a bit more pastel yellow) and a hall dedicated to memorabilia. But even though we grew up with this large-scale celebration in a major American city and are passionate about it, we both know that it can still bear scrutiny.

When Errol decided he would like to chronicle the New Orleans Carnival's more recent past in book form, I became very excited for him and for me. Why? Well, with my job as senior producer at WYES-TV, the primary New Orleans public broadcasting affiliate, and his as editor in chief of *New Orleans Magazine* and three other publications, we have been covering the annual celebration for the last thirty years or so. Writing a new book meant that he would get to reflect on that time and share his insight and knowledge along with his own experiences. He first had the opportunity to analyze Carnival in the early 1970s, when it was the topic of his master's thesis in political science; then in the early 1980s, he wrote the text for *Mardi Gras: A Celebration,* in collaboration with photographer Mitchel Osborne, and he went on to write two more books on the subject. Now Pelican Publishing Company has afforded Errol and Mitchel the opportunity to team up again.

All that said, apart from being married to Errol, I knew that I, as a student of New Orleans Mardi Gras history, wanted to read a new book written by one of the city's foremost Carnival historians, and I felt that others would too.

I especially enjoyed the opportunity to help him present images of modern Carnival. The Muses parade and the Society of St. Anne marching krewe are two examples of contemporary visual pleasures. Thanks to the work of talented photographers as well as the treasures within private collections, The Historic New Orleans Collection, New Orleans Public Library, and Louisiana State Museum, *Mardi Gras: Chronicles of the New Orleans Carnival* showcases images that display the ethereal aspect of New Orleans' pre-Lenten pageant. This task of gathering art was similar to what I undertake when working on a television documentary. And the result is that I get to share with you some real gems.

We New Orleanians are blessed to live in a culture that relishes music, history, and drama and one that comes together every year for a celebration that incorporates all of these and more. The New Orleans Carnival, like the city itself, has always had one foot in the past and one in the present. I'm glad Errol does too.

Peggy Scott Laborde

Preface

Perry Young set the bar; unfortunately he set it impossibly high. The opening two sentences of the preface to his 1931 book, *The Mistick Krewe: Chronicles of Comus and His Kin*, provide the perfect statement about the season: "Carnival is a butterfly of winter, whose last mad flight of Mardi Gras forever ends his glory. Another season is the glory of another butterfly, and the tattered, scattered, fragments of rainbow wings are in turn the record of his day." One can search for other metaphors, but nothing can equal Young's words. Nevertheless, there are plenty of other chores for words to do, and I have tried to put them to work. While this book is visually rich with photography and illustration, I hope that it is a good read, too. Each chapter is structured to provide some historical background (often the result of recent research) as well as stories, lots of stories. A college history professor once explained the rationale behind his anecdote-filled lectures. If the story can get people interested in the topics, "then they will learn more for themselves." Storytelling is a worthy task for words to perform.

Still, the challenge of creating a book is daunting. For that I found solace from an unlikely source: Young himself. While the first two sentences of his preface are heralded, less noticed has been the third, which provides its own bit of wisdom: "In this book the allegory must be remembered, for only fragments are collected." Young concedes that the best he could do was provide snippets of "rainbow wings" and even those are "tattered" and "scattered." The full butterfly remains elusive. Anyone writing about a carnival, especially one as historically and socially complex as it is in New Orleans, will find the fields scattered with fragments.

Collect enough fragments, though, and you will have a whole—if not a butterfly, then potentially a book. This effort looks at Carnival from the perspectives that interest me most, particularly its political and social histories. In doing so, the book brings the season up to date, as it has endured three crises: the 1979 police strike, the 1992 civil rights ordinance controversy, and Hurricane Katrina. Those events left Carnival particularly scattered and tattered, yet the march into the future continues, in many ways stronger than ever.

All new discoveries build on previous findings. While the writing within is original to this book, I have also drawn from the research for some of my earlier writings. In studying Mardi Gras, I have been surprised by how little meaningful research there is, particularly for carnivals and their variants outside New Orleans. There is plenty of misinformation, much of which is now being perpetuated on the Internet. Yet studying the evolution of Mardi Gras gives a glimpse into religion, history, politics, economics, music, folklore, theater, and social structure. It is a rich topic. Human history can be well served once there are more people in the fields chasing butterflies.

For more information on Perry Young, see chapter 2.

Bouquets

Classic social protocol in the world of Carnival calls for the male to venerate the female. The scene is enacted every season when the traditional krewes stage their Carnival balls and the crowd rises at the arrival of the queen and her maids. With the captain overseeing the floor movements and to the polite applause of the audience, man is honoring woman.

If this book were a krewe, the queen would not only be the monarch but the captain, stage manager, and, if needed, tractor driver, as well. To my wife, Peggy Scott Laborde, goes full credit for this book existing. Not only did she provide the needed inspiration but also negotiated the contract, gathered the art, oversaw the production, and prodded when necessary. If there were a floor for her to circle, she would deserve not polite applause but a standing ovation. This book is dedicated to her.

My first chance to have my byline on a cover came in 1981, when photographer Mitchel L. Osborne published a book titled *Mardi Gras: A Celebration.* It was about his stunning photography, but I was honored to be able to provide the text. I will always remember looking out the window over the typewriter and seeing the rising sun after pulling an all-nighter to complete the final chapter.

I am pleased to say that once again Osborne and I are united in print. He was the principal photographer for this project, providing images from his career-long chronicling of Carnival. Many times I have seen him standing on a ladder that was chained to a light pole, leaning precariously to catch the right shot from above the crowd. Once again my paragraphs will be challenged to compete with his art.

In 1997 the leadership of the Rex School of Design offered me the opportunity to write a book to commemorate the krewe's 125th anniversary. They included funding to apply to research, and from that came groundbreaking information. Thanks go to the men of Rex for that opportunity and for contributing to more knowledge about Carnival. Once more, Rex has served his constituents well.

Renaissance Publishing Company has been an important part of my life since it was founded in the wake of Hurricane Katrina. The company, whose many publications include *New Orleans Magazine, Louisiana Life,* and *St. Charles Avenue,* has provided an outlet for Carnival coverage. Thanks to my partners, Todd Matherne and Alan Campell, for keeping the company alive. Thanks also to my co-workers for their good work and for taking seriously their responsibility of bringing a king cake to the office kitchen when one of them gets the baby.

Carnival is so rich in history and imagery that historic photos and illustrations are critical to a book such as this. This publication is enriched by the art gathered from The Historic New Orleans Collection. Big thanks go to Executive Director Priscilla Lawrence for her generosity and support and to researcher supreme

Mary Lou Eichhorn for pointing us in the right direction. We are also grateful for the support of Irene Wainwright, head of the Louisiana Division/City Archives of the New Orleans Public Library.

Although the majority of the photographs are by Mitchel Osborne, when dealing with a cultural celebration as vast as the New Orleans Carnival, it's truly impossible for one person to cover it all. We credit our contributors throughout the book, but special thanks for multiple photographs go to Judi Bottoni, Harriet Cross, Herb Roe, Dr. Stephen Hales, George Long, and Jules Richard IV. Craig Kraemer's assistance in scanning and shooting ephemera is greatly appreciated.

Thanks go to Chefs David Guas, Jeremy Langlois, and Lazone Randolph, along with Lolis Eric Elie and Poppy Tooker for their recipes, and to Bonnie Warren for her organizational efforts.

Since book lengths have limitations, I must here shorten the list, but not without mentioning Pelican Publishing Company. I wish to thank Kathleen Calhoun Nettleton for her confidence in this project and Pelican's Nina Kooij and Terry Callaway for their guiding hands. Additional kudos go to Joseph Billingsley and Scott Campbell, also part of the Pelican family. I owe much gratitude to John Magill for his indexing expertise; *Mardi Gras Guide* publisher Arthur Hardy for his consultation; Eve Kidd Crawford for her editing skills; Doris Ann Gorman for research help; the staff of WYES-TV, Channel 12, and Director of Broadcasting Beth Arroyo Utterback; and Dominic Massa of WWL-TV, Channel 4, whose many duties include coordinating that station's Carnival coverage.

I give special thanks in memory of my parents, Ellis and Rena Laborde, who brought me as an infant to my first Mardi Gras parade, for which I was dressed as a clown.

Finally, to every person whose masquerade has brought humor, beauty, or inspiration to us all—we will never know who you are, but thank you for sharing the spirit.

Mardi Gras

CHRONICLES OF THE NEW ORLEANS CARNIVAL

CHAPTER 1

Twelfth Night Reveling

HISTORIC WANDERINGS

The Man Who Made Twelfth Night Famous

A winter night in England, probably an evening when a warm wassail and a light comedy could provide relief from the cold and dampness of the new year: what happened that evening would lead to Twelfth Night, January 6, a date that would be celebrated in a city not on the Thames but on the mightier Mississippi River, on the far side of the Atlantic. This particular evening, though, was February 2, 1602. The location was London's Middle Temple Court. A new play attributed to the popular William Shakespeare premiered. It was called *Twelfth Night*.

French history painter Thomas Couture recreates a pagan festival similar to the Saturnalia in his Romans During the Decadence *(1847). This festivity was considered a wilder precursor to our Carnival celebration.* (Courtesy of the Musee D'Orsay)

Dutch-born British painter Sir Lawrence Alma-Tadema's Ave Caesar, Io Saturnalia! *(1880) depicts a Roman winter festival that is believed to be a forerunner to early Carnival celebrations.* (Courtesy of the Akron Art Museum)

There is nothing to the play that suggests the celebration of the holiday other than some wacky cross-dressing scenes, a motif carried out in other Shakespeare plays such as *As You Like It*, but gender-bending was in the spirit of the annual post-Christmas rituals from which Twelfth Night, the day, ascended. (In mentioning Shakespeare, we are aware that debate continues as to whether he actually wrote the works attributed him. For our purposes, his name is used in reference to the body of works published under his name, regardless of whom the author, if not him, might have been.)

Twelfth Night, the holiday, emerged from the various pre-Christian celebrations. During the cold months that characterized the change from one year to the other, when the days grew shorter and agriculture and fieldwork had ceased until the spring, winter became a time for lighting fires for illumination and partying with some of the bounty from the growing season. There was a feeling of abandon from the stresses of life, giving rise to a character known as the Lord of Misrule, who was a symbol of the world turned upside down. Peasants would dress as royalty; royalty would dress as peasants. (Variations of this theme would carry on into modern Mardi Gras. In several places, a straw dummy, likely descended from the Lord of Misrule, is burned as Carnival ends, just as Misrule reigned until the stroke of midnight each Twelfth Night.)

Peasants Celebrating Twelfth Night, by Flemish artist David Teniers II, gives a hint of the raucous celebration of Twelfth Night in the 1600s. (Courtesy of the National Gallery of Art)

Pagan Rome celebrated the season with the Saturnalia; Celts lit bonfires for their Samhain (a predecessor to today's Halloween). England, during the Tudor reign, bridged the dark months by celebrating from Allhallows Eve through Christmas and until Twelfth Night. Christians declared the twelfth day of Christmas to be the Feast of Epiphany, the day that the newborn Christ was recognized to be God. How that happened varied from church sect to sect, but the Western churches associated the date with the visit of the Magi.

(One bit of confusion was which date was Twelfth Night. In some places it was celebrated on January 5, in others on January 6. If Christmas night, December

A mid-nineteenth-century newspaper illustration of revelers celebrating Carnival in Rome could easily depict New Orleans during that time (From the collection of Peggy Scott Laborde)

25, is celebrated as the "first" night of Christmas—a logical assumption—then the twelfth night would be January 5. If the counting starts on the twenty-sixth, then the sixth would be the date. Over time January 6 won out, and, like so much else in church-related math, sometimes it is easier just to accept what survives and move on.)

Throughout most of the world, Twelfth Night is a minor holiday, and it would be in New Orleans too had it not been for Shakespeare. In 1870 a group of young men in New Orleans founded a parading organization to be called the Twelfth Night Revelers. Their parade and soirée would be held on January 6, the first day of the Carnival season. At the time there was only one other parade, the Mistick Krewe of Comus, which paraded on the evening of Mardi Gras, the last night of the Carnival season. It is likely—in fact, practically inevitable—that the men who founded the Twelfth Night Revelers were in the same social circles as the Comus crowd. Indeed, just as Comus members would be involved in establishing Rex in 1872, there was almost definitely a Comus influence on the Twelfth Night Revelers.

Founding parades, like owning racehorses, was not a poor man's pastime. It took money and connections. The men who founded the Revelers would

Twelfth Day Celebration *in Havana from the* Illustrated London News, *late 1840s.*
(From the collection of Peggy and Errol Laborde)

have been part of the town's educated elite, schooled in the classic literature of the time. In creating Comus, the founders borrowed from a masque (a form of courtly entertainment often involving singing, dancing, and acting) of the same name written by British poet John Milton that had premiered in London's Ludlow castle in 1634. Just as Shakespeare's *Twelfth Night* was written in celebration of a Christian holiday, so too was *Comus*, which premiered on a day then known as Michaelmas—the feast of St. Michael the Archangel. Its date, September 29, was conveniently close to the equinox and thus recognized as a harbinger of autumn and shortened days.

From the date that the Twelfth Night Revelers, or TNR, stepped out into the world, January 6, 1870, they put their own spin on the day. Borrowing from pre-Christian antecedents, the monarch would be known as the Lord of Misrule. The pagan practice of serving a pastry on that day would be ritualized in the form of a cake from which maids would draw beans attached to ribbons; the one who got the gold bean would be queen. The tableau ball held after the parade borrowed from the traditions of European royalty. Although the TNR Ball survives, after several reorganizations, the Revelers parade did not. The last street parade of the original Twelfth Night Revelers was in 1876. (Much of the information about early Carnival balls

Two ball goers gaze at each other in the midst of some frantic reveling during an 1858 Carnival ball in Paris. (From the collection of Peggy Scott Laborde)

Thanks to the French publication Illustration, Journal Universal, *in 1858, this scene from a Carnival ball in Paris shows us what balls in New Orleans might have looked like, but on a smaller scale.* (From the collection of Peggy Scott Laborde)

comes from the 1952 book *New Orleans Masquerade: Chronicles of Carnival,* by Arthur Burton LaCour. This is one of the most important volumes ever written about the New Orleans Carnival. Like this book, it was published by Pelican Publishing Company. We are proud to be in such good company.)

From the themes of the first few parades, we can learn something of the group's influences. While the premiere 1870 march had no particular message, the second parade borrowed from Britain with "Mother Goose's Tea Party." The 1872 theme may have been the most revealing—"English Humor."

When he took time off to relax, the Lord of Misrule, I suspect, reveled in the words of Shakespeare.

This 1884 Twelfth Night Revelers invitation illustrates the krewe's "Kingdom of Flowers" theme. The ball was held at the French Opera House. (Courtesy of the Louisiana Division/City Archives, New Orleans Public Library)

"Audubon and His Creations" was the theme of the Twelfth Night Revelers tableau in 1873. During the ball, krewe members would pose onstage in various scenes depicting the chosen theme. (Courtesy of The Historic New Orleans Collection)

A "Norseman" converses with two masked ladies during an 1858 Parisian Carnival ball. (From the collection of Peggy Scott Laborde)

At the Twelfth Night Revelers Ball, maids of the court draw tiny boxes from a giant "cake." Each box contains a silver bean, except for one, which holds a gold bean and designates the queen of the ball. (Photo © Mitchel Osborne)

This gold bean is drawn by the queen of the Twelfth Night Revelers Ball. (Courtesy of The Historic New Orleans Collection)

The 2013 Proteus parade paid tribute to some of the more historic New Orleans Carnival organizations. This float celebrates the Twelfth Night Revelers. (Photo © Judi Bottoni)

STORIES TOLD

Phollowing the Phellows

On Twelfth Night, a mysterious group would gather their trench coats, float riders' masks, a cowbell or two, and hand-printed signs and head to the Willow Street streetcar barn. Once disguised, they would congregate near the spot where the Phunny Phorty Phellows were preparing for their annual January 6 streetcar ride to announce the Carnival season's arrival. One member of the group would start ringing the cowbell, and others held the signs; soon members of the Phellows would be drawn to the maskers, whose identities they did not know. Over the years an informal routine evolved. "I didn't catch your names," a Phellow would usually say, to which the maskers would reply with names of Carnival krewes past and present, such as Mecca, Okeanos, and Proteus. The signs they carried were satirical, some with a biting wit, some with an eerie inside knowledge of the Phellows' organizers.

An admit card to an 1896 ball held by the original Phunny Phorty Phellows. The krewe's symbol was an owl; note the owl-wing design. (From the collection of Peggy Scott Laborde)

Once the Phellows' streetcar ride began, the "Mystery Maskers," as the Phellows referred to them, would disappear, showing up again at other spots

For many years the Phunny Phorty Phellows have announced their Twelfth Night streetcar ride in the form of a proclamation. This one was designed by New Orleans artist Arthur Nead. (From the collection of Peggy Scott Laborde)

along the route, each time with different signs. Then one year a Masker straddled the streetcar tracks as the trolley approached Gallier Hall. His sign boldly commanded the streetcar to stop. It did, and thus began an annual ritual of Phellow officialdom and the Maskers toasting each other in front of the former city hall. It was the first toast of the season at the site where parade royalty would toast other officials as Carnival unfolded.

No toast was as genuine. The Maskers brought champagne. The Phellows disembarked the streetcar and offered praise. One year the Maskers gave the Phellows a proclamation commanding that a plaque be placed on the corner of Julia and Magazine streets, identifying it as the spot where, in 1857, the first Comus parade began, launching the Carnival parading tradition. The Maskers' ritual was always brief. Within moments, Phellow officialdom was climbing back into the streetcar, but not before one Phellow, always moved by the occasion, would tell the Maskers, "Y'all are the real thing; you represent the true spirit of Carnival."

Two officials of the Phunny Phorty Phellows. (From the collection of Peggy Scott Laborde)

While the original krewe of the Phunny Phorty Phellows was all male, this is no longer the case. The PPP, as it was known, paraded from 1878 off and on for almost twenty years. It was revived in 1981. (Photo by George Long)

Right before the Phunny Phorty Phellows board the St. Charles Avenue streetcar on Twelfth Night, the captain and outgoing monarchs cut a ribbon to officially proclaim the beginning of the Carnival season. The group is toasted by officials from the Krewe of Oak. (Photo by Jules Richard IV)

The Storyville Stompers perform during the Phunny Phorty Phellows streetcar ride on Twelfth Night. (Photo © Mitchel Osborne)

Everyone on the Phunny Phorty Phellows' Twelfth Night streetcar ride must be costumed and masked. (Photo © Mitchel Osborne)

The Phunny Phorty Phellows' streetcar travels for one block on Canal Street before heading back uptown. (Photo © Mitchel Osborne)

Maskers at the Phunny Phorty Phellows Coronation Ball pay tribute to a beloved local pastry. (Photo by Peggy Scott Laborde)

Harold Myers, Jr., organizer of the Mystery Maskers, was among Carnival's biggest fans. (Photo by Peggy Scott Laborde)

After the streetcar began moving again, the Maskers would appear a few more times along the route, with their last sighting being outside the streetcar barn. Then they would vanish into the night, not to be seen or heard from until the next Twelfth Night. The ritual evolved over the years, and amazingly, no one in the Phellows ever knew who the Maskers were.

I was checking my phone at JFK Airport when I found the message. A saddened voice asked me to contact him, saying that he had disturbing news about someone I had never met but with whom I was familiar. That's when I heard Harold Myers, Jr.'s name for the first time. A cousin of his told me that Myers loved Carnival in New Orleans, and he celebrated it in a way unlike anyone else: as part of the Mystery Maskers. He then informed me that on the previous evening, Myers had been returning home from a New Orleans Zephyrs baseball game. His automobile was near Bonnabel Boulevard and the I-10 Service Road when a stolen truck being pursued by police crashed into him.

Myers did not ride in a krewe and never reigned as a king, but he did capture the spirit and integrity of the season as though chosen by its spirits. The spirit was now gone. His family's tragedy was also one of Twelfth Night's great losses.

"Harold loved virtually everything about New Orleans, the people, the food, the culture, the history, and often remarked that this city was unlike any other city in the world," one of his cousins wrote me. "He was emblematic of everything that was right about the city of New Orleans and unfortunately died being a tragic symbol of everything that was wrong with the city of New Orleans."

I later learned that Myers worked for the Louisiana Department of Labor's Job Services division, where he was known for showing real compassion for outcasts and creating opportunities for them. A friend lamented that he would have wanted to find a job for the person who was driving the stolen truck.

In 2009 Zulu and his queen, who were celebrating that group's centennial, were among the Phellows' guests on the streetcar ride. Extending his hand through a streetcar window, Myers offered the Zulu royalty a cup of champagne. It would be his last Twelfth Night toast. At that time, he was told that the plaque he had proclaimed into existence years earlier now stood on Magazine and Julia streets. Although it speaks of Comus, the plaque is truly a tribute to someone who was moved by the season in a way that few people understood.

Myers lived in Metairie, but his funeral Mass was at St. John the Baptist Catholic Church in Central City, which, a cousin said, was his favorite church. "Why a church so far away from home?" I asked. "Because," the cousin answered, "it was close to the parade route."

King Cake: A Quieter Ritual

In places where Carnival is not practiced, Twelfth Night is just another winter evening, but in New Orleans, it is alive with subtle native rituals. Since

The Mystery Maskers follow the Phunny Phorty Phellows during their ride with satirical comments on Carnival. (Photo © Mitchel Osborne)

1870, the Twelfth Night Revelers have (with only occasional gaps) held their society ball on that evening, quietly and privately recognizing the season. On that same evening, the Phellows have taken to a streetcar. The banners tied to the side announce to the world, or at least to those waiting for a trolley, that "It's Carnival Time!" TV news coverage of the ride has become for some people the harbinger of the season. As Carnival has grown and become marketed and manipulated, and in an age when some krewes offer positions on their floats in visitor packages, much of the mystery, magic, and spontaneity have been lost. But in the dawning hours of each Carnival season, the spirit manifests itself.

Carnival has suffered losses through the years, but a city with endangered traditions at least has more soul than a city with no traditions at all. Among those traditions is the king cake. Carnival's beginning, Twelfth Night, is a fixed date, but its ending, midnight on Mardi Gras, is movable, meaning that the number of days of being exposed to king cake varies from year to year. The cakes show up almost everywhere during the season. Once they were baked so dry and undistinguished that they were easy to ignore. Now, injected with various flavors of globby tempting stuff, they can bust any New Year's diet resolutions. Few confections are as rich in rituals as they are in calories.

At the Twelfth Night Revelers Ball, an enormous artificial king cake is rolled

Whoever receives the slice of king cake with the plastic baby in it is crowned the Phellows' monarch, traditionally called the Boss. (Photo by George Long)

This masker has just discovered he has been chosen Boss of the Phunny Phorty Phellows. (Photo by Jules Richard IV)

out. "Slices" are served to the waiting debutantes. Each "slice" contains a silver bean except one. The young lady who receives the gold bean becomes queen. For the Phunny Phorty Phellows, wobbling along on a streetcar, real king cakes are used to determine the royalty for that year. One year, the queen-select was so excited that, after the ride, she called her out-of-town father to announce the news. The last time he had heard from her was when she had called to complain that the pipes in her home had been burst by a recent freeze. On this Twelfth Night, the old man, not used to the ways of New Orleans, seemed confused by his daughter's announcement. "Oh, so you're clean?" he inquired. "No," the daughter replied. "I didn't say I'm 'clean'; I said I'm 'queen.'" Pity those places where, on January 6, it is more important to be clean than to be queen. In New Orleans, we know better.

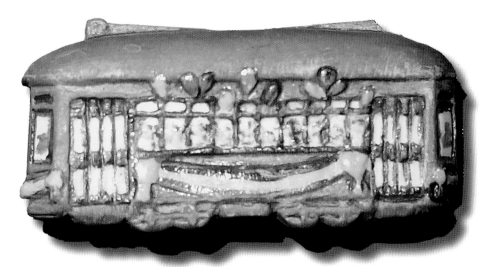

Haydel's Bakery has offered various symbols of Carnival in its king cakes that are reminiscent of the porcelain "feves" or trinkets found inside king cakes in the nineteenth century. This one represents the Phunny Phorty Phellows' Twelfth Night streetcar ride. (From the collection of Peggy Scott Laborde)

CHAPTER 2

Comus and Rex

HISTORIC WANDERINGS

The Man Who Would Be King

Whenever Rex rides on his gold-bedecked float, it would be a historically gracious gesture if he would nod his head and wave his scepter to the left along the 200 block of St. Charles Avenue. That stretch of street is now occupied by the Place St. Charles office building, but within it is the ghost of the St. Charles Hotel, which once stood at that site. If one spot can be pinpointed as the birthplace of the Rex organization, it would be there.

Rex was a monarch born during a time when the politics of democracy were torn by Reconstruction. With all of Louisiana's outrageous and even notorious politics that would follow in the next century, no year was quite as politically outrageous and notorious as Reconstruction-ravaged 1872, when two separate governments were installed. Bloodshed would ensue. Rex was born not because of the politics but in spite of them. And as new research has shown, though he

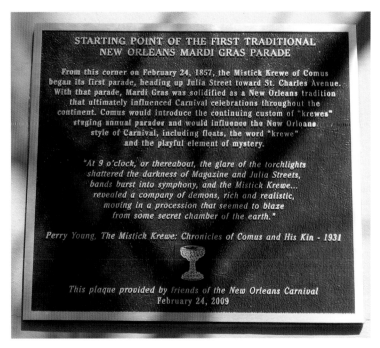

In 1857 the Mistick Krewe of Comus began its first parade, from the corner of Julia and Magazine streets. This plaque commemorates the group that created the first organized parade, so much a part of the New Orleans Carnival. (Photo by Peggy Scott Laborde)

Comus created the concept of a parade that other parades of the New Orleans Carnival have followed. (Photo © Mitchel Osborne)

Comus being toasted at the Pickwick Club. The Mistick Krewe of Comus paraded from 1857 until 1991. (Photo © Mitchel Osborne)

A playful homage to Comus, the mythological figure known for carrying a cup of potent libation and the namesake of the first organized New Orleans parading Carnival krewe. (Photo © Mitchel Osborne)

was a monarch, his mission, at least by the standards of the day, was democratic.

By 1872 some of New Orleans' business leaders and journalists were anxious to promote the city again to the rest of the country. Carnival created marketable opportunities. At the time, the only public presentation on Mardi Gras was the march of the Mistick Krewe of Comus. But Comus paraded at night; a day parade was needed to nurture Mardi Gras and to open participation beyond Comus's limited membership. Comus was supportive of the new parade. Its captain and some of its members lent their expertise to create Rex, who advertised for public participation in his procession.

Rex, who was born with a public purpose, coupled with Comus, whose purpose was social, in effect made an event worthy of attracting tourists. The fact that the Russian Grand Duke Alexis Romanoff happened to be in town at the time of the first Rex parade romanticized the royal birth. The duke's presence would eclipse the less poetic but more practical fact that the monarch was conceived partially to help rev up the economy.

Alexis, who stayed at the St. Charles Hotel during his New Orleans visit, would become an enduring figure in Rex lore. But among the other young men who met in the chambers of the St. Charles Hotel to plan the first parade was a lineage that research has, until now, largely overlooked—American royalty.

Cotton merchant Lewis Salomon served as the first Rex. Little has been written about him other than that he was Jewish. (That fact we traditionally treated with a certain irony, given Carnival's Christian origins. However,

A float from a Comus parade in the 1980s entering Armstrong Park and heading toward the Municipal Auditorium for the ball following the parade. Comus last paraded in 1991. (Photo © Mitchel Osborne)

research for a February 2004 *New Orleans Magazine* article revealed that in 1862, in the same week that he joined the Confederate army, Salomon converted to Catholicism. He would spend most of his life as a devout and philanthropic Catholic, though his burial site would be a Jewish cemetery in Brooklyn.)

Salomon was born in Mobile, Alabama, but his roots trace back to Philadelphia, home of his great-great-grandfather Haym Salomon. Here was a man who was a glorious footnote to American history. We hear of generals and politicians but seldom of those who pay for the wars. Haym Salomon was one of the chief financiers of the American Revolution and a friend of George Washington. (In Chicago, there is even a statue of Haym, who lost his fortunes and died in debt, standing alongside Washington and Robert Morris, a financial adviser of the general's.)

One of the key people in creating Rex was a young newspaperman, E. C. Hancock, who lived at the St. Charles Hotel. He was from Philadelphia and a descendent of John Hancock. It is quite likely that John Hancock and Haym Salomon, the great relatives of two of Rex's founders, knew each other.

The organizers of the first Rex parade met at the nationally famous St. Charles Hotel to plan the procession. (Courtesy of The Historic New Orleans Collection)

Just like Haym, Lewis Salomon became the fundraiser for a cause. He pulled together the money for the Rex parade. In different centuries, both the Hancocks and the Salomons had a hand in creating new sovereignties.

St. Charles Avenue was the hub of economic and social life in the New Orleans of 1872. Along its path are other ghosts for Rex to toast. At the site of the InterContinental New Orleans Hotel, where Rex now toasts his queen, once stood two theaters, the Academy of Music and the St. Charles Theater. During the time of Mardi Gras 1872, two nationally known performers were appearing next door to each other: Lydia Thompson at the Academy of Music; Lotta Crabtree at the St. Charles Theater. Both would become a part of the Grand Duke saga.

New Orleans businessman Lewis Salomon was the first Rex, King of Carnival. Rex initially rode on horseback, as depicted by artist George Schmidt in his painting, First Rex, 1872. (Courtesy of George Schmidt)

This stereoscope shows what is believed to be the first Rex parade, in 1872, as it turned from Canal Street onto St. Charles Street. (If so, it is the only known photograph of that parade.) Though archives identify the photo as having been taken in 1866, that is likely a mistake, since there was no day parade of that magnitude prior to Rex. Riders are wearing Bedouin costumes known to be worn in that parade. Note the size of the crowd and that the tradition of spectators wearing costumes had not been established yet. (Courtesy of the Louisiana State Museum)

Romantic Rumors

Carnival's most romantic legend is that of the Grand Duke Alexis and burlesque singer Lydia Thompson. (Burlesque in those days did not mean strippers but more of a satirical, only slightly naughty, leggy entertainment.) As the story goes, "If Ever I Cease to Love" became Carnival's anthem when it was learned that Alexis was smitten with Lydia. He had heard her sing that song when they had both happened to be in St. Louis. There he had seen her perform *Bluebeard,* a show that contained several numbers including that one. Through an envoy, Alexis had even sent Lydia a bracelet. The legend continues that the bands in the first Rex parade, having heard of Alexis's fondness for Lydia and the song, played "If Ever I Cease to Love" as they marched past the duke. This tale served as a plot device in Rex's origin myth—not just a love story but one matching royalty with a showgirl.

Now for the truth. Alexis may have become infatuated while in New Orleans, although with a different woman. Lotta Crabtree, who at age twenty-five had already won fame performing in the gold-rush camps near San Francisco, made a return engagement to New Orleans. On this trip she was presenting a show called *The Little Duchess,* at the St. Charles Theater. Alexis attended Crabtree's performance. He was so charmed that he sent an aide to express his congratulations to the actress. The duke had also accepted a well-publicized invitation to see Lydia Thompson's show, which he missed, opting to stay at the Jockey Club, where luncheon activities ran into the evening.

Overlooked in the Lydia-Alexis romance theory is the significant age difference between the two. Alexis was twenty-two; Lydia was thirty-six. If

Grand Duke Alexis's visit to New Orleans during the 1872 Carnival added luster to the celebration. (Photo by Sergei Lvovich Levitsky, courtesy of Wikipedia Commons)

The Grand Duke Alexis watched the first Rex parade and, later that day, the Comus parade. Note the smoke created by flambeaux in this oil painting, The Grand Duke Alexis Watching the Comus Parade. (Courtesy of George Schmidt)

The Rex Den, photographed by John Tibule Mendes in 1901. Located on Calliope Street near the Mississippi River, it burned in 1950. (Courtesy of The Historic New Orleans Collection)

The current Rex float den in Central City. (Photo by Peggy Scott Laborde)

Rex floats are lined up in the den in preparation for the parade. (Photo by Peggy Scott Laborde)

The Boeuf Gras (fatted calf), representing the feasting before the fasting of Lent, has long been a sign of Carnival, with French origins. Here artist Boyd Cruise shows the 1882 Rex parade. (Courtesy of The Historic New Orleans Collection)

The Rex parade featured a live Boeuf Gras in its procession until 1901. Here is a rare view of the animal atop a float the year before. (From the collection of Peggy Scott Laborde)

A close-up view of the Boeuf Gras float from the 1900 Rex parade. (From the collection of Peggy Scott Laborde)

Lydia had a friend among those who were part of Rex's first day, it may not have been a duke but a king. Thompson's 1872 visit to New Orleans was her third tour here, so she was well known in the community. Lewis Salomon, Rex I, was active in theater. He would have had many opportunities to make her acquaintance.

A curious statement published in the *New Orleans Times* on February 6, 1872, a week before Mardi Gras, revealed the first Rex as being a ruler with love on his mind. A series of tongue-in-cheek articles, likely written by E. C. Hancock, had been printed, each telling about the mysterious "King of Carnival" preparing for his debut. The article that day even dealt with the king's social life:

His majesty has never married, giving as an excuse that this state should not be entered into until experience has sobered the liveliness of youth and all the wild oats have been sown. We give this latter piece of information for the benefit of the ladies who are already overwhelming His Majesty. . . .
It is well to note in the latter connection that the national air or anthem of the Carnival Dynasty, for many centuries past, has been, as is at present, "If ever I cease to love."

Besides its playfulness, the statement is significant because it disproves the legend that "If Ever I Cease to Love" spontaneously evolved as Carnival's anthem when bands began to play it for the duke in 1872. As early as a week before, the song was already proclaimed as the anthem.

The truth is that the song preceded Lydia to New Orleans. According to Arthur Hardy's 1989 *Mardi Gras Guide*, the song, which was first published in London in 1867, was written by a certain George Leybourne, whose other big hit was "The Man on the Flying Trapeze." Depending on where it was performed, the lyrics were changed, quite often to be local and topical (e.g., "may the Grand Duke Alexis ride a buffalo through Texas") but always expressing an undying love. In 1871, Thompson adapted the song for her burlesque, *Bluebeard.* In that same year, the song was published in at least two songbooks: the *If Ever I Cease to Love Songster* and the *Half-Dime Series of Choice Music.* With that, the song spread throughout the country. New Orleans, a port city with a vibrant theater community, would have been among the first places to receive new music.

A poem published in the *Times* on November 6, 1871, makes it evident that the song was popular in New Orleans more than three months before Rex's premiere:

A SONG FOR SENTIMENTALISTS
(Not a bit more silly than some we have heard lately.)

If never I cease to love,
The moon may change her hue,
And 'mid the stars above
The sun no more burn blue.

Among the woodland trees,
The whales their song may cease,
And oysters at their ease,
May keep their beds in peace.

If never I cease to love,
The cows may catch the croup,
While of the turtle dove,
Lord mayors no more make soup.
The frogs may plow the main,
The tigers soar far above,
The rain may cease to reign,
If never I cease to love.

The theme of the 1900 Rex parade was Terpsichore, the muse of dance in ancient Greek mythology. Note the brass band in front of the title float. Many of these bands would have been playing popular marches of the day, including compositions by John Philip Sousa. Ironically, the float den was located on Calliope Street, named for the muse of music. (From the collection of Peggy Scott Laborde)

Chances are Hancock wrote the poem, obviously a spoof of the published version of the song. To Hancock, its playful lyrics might have seemed perfect for Carnival.

"If Ever I Cease to Love," contrary to legend, was not played for the duke during the Rex parade. For him, the bands performed the Russian national anthem. The song was played instead for the King of Carnival, at his reviewing stand. Auguste Davis, a New Orleans music teacher, developed a march arrangement for the song, enabling the bands in the original Rex parade to follow the decree that the tune should be performed while "passing in review before His Majesty."

The Grand Duke began his Mardi Gras evening by watching the Mistick Krewe of Comus parade along the city's old streets as though drawing a curtain on the Carnival season. Alexis attended the Comus Ball at the Varieties theater, then moved on to the Academy of Music. On other nights, the popular Lydia Thompson was appearing here, but this night a group called *La Coterie Carnaval* staged a Grand Bal Déguisé. Alexis was greeted with the Russian national anthem. From there he attended another ball, this one at the St. Charles Theater, where he was reported to have stayed until two o'clock of Ash Wednesday morning. The *Times* was so moved by the day's events, which had begun with Rex, that it boasted in its Wednesday edition of "a new era in the long history of Mardi Gras festivities." The newspaper added that "the advent has not only been brilliant, but successful," to which "the thousands of delighted people who were not slow to express their enthusiasm can fully testify."

Homemade costumes were popular during the early 1900s. (Photo by Alexander Allison, courtesy of the Louisiana Division/City Archives, New Orleans Public Library)

Rex did not stage a Carnival ball in its first year. Many of the organization's founders probably attended the Comus Ball that evening. Rex himself, his reign over and now a civilian in the person of Lewis Salomon, most likely spent the evening at the Academy of Music. He was listed as a "Manager" of *La Coterie Carnaval* as well as a member of its invitation committee. Salomon and the Grand Duke quite likely met at the ball that night, although we will never know if Alexis was aware he was meeting Rex. The identity of the first Rex had been kept secret throughout that Mardi Gras.

Possibly in that number at *La Coterie*'s ball was Lydia Thompson, who, because of the ball, would have had the night off from her gig at the Academy. If Alexis did greet Lydia at the ball, however, it was probably the only time he saw her in New Orleans, for, legends to the contrary, the Grand Duke royally snubbed her.

Businessman John E. Koerner III reigned as Rex in 2008. (Photo © Mitchel Osborne)

Rex now features a Boeuf Gras made of papier-mâché as one of its signature floats. (Photo by Errol Laborde)

Actress Lotta Crabtree caught the eye of the Grand Duke Alexis while he was in town.

A romance between popular British-born entertainer Lydia Thompson and the Grand Duke Alexis may be the stuff of legend, but their New Orleans visit kept the local papers busy. (From the Arthur Hardy Collection)

A dance card from the 1899 Comus Ball. Note the attached pencil. (From the collection of Peggy Scott Laborde)

Sovereign to Sovereign

While the importance of the Grand Duke Alexis's presence at the first Rex parade has long been overstated, it should not be totally diminished. Alexis was a catalyst. His coming gave reason to hasten a parade that might have happened anyway. The duke did view the parade at Gallier Hall, and his presence added true royalty to the event. He may have even increased parade attendance among those who were curious to see him see the parade. His appearance on Mardi Gras 1872 romanticized Rex and perhaps legitimized Rex's claim to be the King of Carnival—one sovereign acknowledging another.

The duke legend would have it that the Rex parade was intended to be a onetime event to honor the visitor. However, Hancock's own paper, the *Times*, was uncertain where the duke would be Mardi Gras afternoon. In its February 7 edition, six days before Mardi Gras, the newspaper reported that the duke would see the Comus parade at Lafayette Square and added the following: "One of the numerous clubs on Canal Street will no doubt tender the use of a verandah, should the Grand Duke desire to see the revel of the King of the Carnival."

Alexis's legends survive only because Rex thrives. Without the krewe, the duke would be long forgotten, as he is in his native Russia.

A public official of far lesser rank from a much smaller place may have had a greater influence on Rex's evolution. In 1866, a city clerk in Mobile, Alabama, named Joe Cain spearheaded a disorganized parade designed to poke fun at the federal occupiers. His procession became known as the People's Parade. Joe Cain Day is still celebrated in Mobile on the Sunday before Mardi Gras.

By 1872, there seemed to be growing pressure for a people's parade in New Orleans, too, not one as informal or rebellious as Cain's but one that would expand participation in Carnival. The history of Carnival in the Gulf South is like a rock thrown into a pool. The impact causes a series of circles, each spreading a little farther. *Carnival American Style: Mardi Gras at New Orleans and Mobile*, a scholarly book by history professor Sam Kinser, offered a startling observation: "Comus was incomplete without Rex. The private-society idea needed a civic dimension in order to survive in a democratically organized polity."

That is not at all a criticism of Comus, for some Rex founders also belonged to the Mistick Krewe. The infant Rex was nourished by Comus expertise. (William Merriam, one of the key Rex founders, was a Comus captain.) But it was in the nature of Comus and the mystic organizations in Mobile to be private, not only internally but externally, as well. Carnival needed a persona, a public figure, a benevolent monarch. Although many Rex members traveled in the same high-society circles as those in the mystic clubs, Rex would play a more civic role. Consider the words written by Perry Young in *The Mistick Krewe*, which, though published fifty-nine years before Kinser, expressed a similar sentiment: "The fame of Comus had spread and was drawing crowds of visitors from afar, to the great embarrassment of the Krewe, whose entertainments were designed for the amusement of themselves and their immediate friends. Another society was needed."

A frank and revealing newspaper report that sounds like something written in modern New Orleans spelled out the tourism purpose. The February 11, 1872, issue of the *Republican*, published

An invitation to the 1924 Comus Ball. (From the collection of Peggy Scott Laborde)

two days before Mardi Gras of that year and Rex's debut, stated:

> We have published the several edicts issued by Rex, so our readers are posted on his intention. One of the foremost considerations in this display is to make our city attractive, not entirely for citizens, but principally for visitors. Items of these things have gone abroad, and public attention has been drawn to New Orleans. This will bring hither not less than 15,000 people, and they will, on a low average, expend fifty dollars each, thus bringing capital to our city.

Building to a crescendo, the *Republican* continued:

> Every visitor, on returning home, will give his less fortunate neighbors a pleasant or glowing account of the wonders of the Crescent City. Next year the number of visitors will be doubled; and so our city will be benefitted. For this reason residents should make the celebration as attractive as possible, and Rex has pursued the right course.

A Comus captain from the 1940s. While the Rex captain wears gold, the Comus captain is in silver and white. (From the collection of Peggy Scott Laborde)

"Maskers (George Washington style)" are shown in this photo taken by John Tibule Mendes on Mardi Gras Day, circa 1920. (Courtesy of The Historic New Orleans Collection)

A trio of lady maskers on Canal Street in the early 1920s, as photographed by John Tibule Mendes. (Courtesy of The Historic New Orleans Collection)

A masker strikes a whimsical pose on Canal Street circa the 1920s, as captured by John Tibule Mendes. (Courtesy of The Historic New Orleans Collection)

Top left: *Rex stops for a toast at Gallier Hall in this photo by John Tibule Mendes, circa 1920. (Courtesy of The Historic New Orleans Collection)*

Middle left: *St. Charles Avenue has long been part of the Rex parade route, as shown in this photo from the early 1900s by John Tibule Mendes. (Courtesy of The Historic New Orleans Collection)*

Bottom left: *The Duke and Duchess of Windsor visited New Orleans during the 1950 Mardi Gras. They are shown here with Mayor deLesseps "Chep" Morrison in the reviewing stands at Gallier Hall during the Rex parade. (Courtesy of the Louisiana Division/City Archives, New Orleans Public Library)*

Maskers on Carnival Day, 1923, as photographed by John Tibule Mendes. Note the homemade costumes. (Courtesy of The Historic New Orleans Collection)

Gallier Hall, formerly New Orleans' City Hall, has long been a ceremonial stop during Carnival parades. This photo by John Tibule Mendes shows Mayor Martin Behrman and little Lucille Newlin welcoming Rex on February 19, 1917. (Courtesy of The Historic New Orleans Collection)

Many kings have come to power with less civic calling than did Rex. On the practical side, Rex gave the New Orleans Carnival a day parade. That in turn had financial benefits for the city, as circulars promoting New Orleans and its expanded Carnival were distributed by the railroads along their route. On the civic side, Rex allowed greater participation in Carnival. On the political side, Rex gave Carnival a public figure in counterpoint to the cherished secrecy of the mystic clubs. On the ceremonial side, Rex greeted a grand duke.

Kingdoms are created by circumstance, but few can count among their circumstances one that Rex could. His kingdom came into existence partially because democracy of that day demanded it. There would be many more krewes and many more kings to follow in future years.

On November 18, 1908, a procession moved along the Champs-Elysées in Paris. With full military escort, the body of the Grand Duke Alexis was taken from his home in Paris to a

Each year Rex presents a parade with all original floats. (Photo © Mitchel Osborne)

Russian church, where a funeral service lasted nearly two hours, and then to the Gare du Nord railroad station, from which a special train would take Alexis to St. Petersburg. By bizarre coincidence, six days later, in London, a funeral service was held for Mrs. Alex Henderson, whom the world had better known as the actress Lydia Thompson. Lost in the obituaries was the role the two had played thirty-six years earlier in the birth of a kingdom in New Orleans. Their paths had gone in different directions, but during their lives Lydia and Alexis were the subject of love stories both real and imagined.

Kings being immortal, Rex still marches to the anthem declared by edict for his 1872 debut. As it is played, the legends of Alexis and Lydia survive for, history aside, in the kingdom of Carnival, they never ceased to love.

Henri Schindler, artistic director for the Rex parade, draws inspiration from the early designers of this historic parade. (Photo © Mitchel Osborne)

Rex maskers wear brightly colored costumes. (Photo by Peggy Scott Laborde)

The Citadel Summerall Guards drill team is a familiar sight in the Rex parade each year. (Photo by Peggy Scott Laborde)

Artist H. Alvin Sharpe approached the Rex organization about the prospect of his designing a Rex doubloon. The doubloon made its debut in 1960 and would become a Carnival sensation. (Photo © Mitchel Osborne)

Truck-float krewes, such as the Elks Krewe of Orleanians and the Krewe of Crescent City, have followed Rex on Carnival Day since the 1940s. (Courtesy of the Louisiana Division/City Archives, New Orleans Public Library)

Since 1988, Sr. Olivia Wassmer, a Poor Clare nun, has created ornaments depicting scenes from the New Orleans Carnival. Proceeds go to support the order. (From the collection of Peggy Scott Laborde)

Rex and his queen participate in a "Royal Run" each Mardi Gras morning at Audubon Park. From left in foreground: William H. Hines, Rex 2013, Nina O'Brien Sloss, queen of Rex 2013, and Christian Brown, a Rex official. (Photo by Justin Winston)

William H. Hines, left, toasts his queen, Nina O'Brien Sloss, and her parents at Rex's "Royal Run." Shown in the blue Rex cap is William Boater Reily III, who reigned as Rex in 1982 and founded the run. Next to him is Price Lanier, race coordinator. (Photo by Justin Winston)

STORIES TOLD

A Butterfly of Winter

There are many rituals during the Comus Ball on Mardi Gras evening, including one originated by the television crew covering the event. As Comus, Rex, and their queens circle the floor, with the "Grand March" from *Aida* played in the background, someone recites to the TV audience the opening sentences to the preface of a classic Carnival book by Perry Young. No monarch has ever spoken nor bard ever written a more eloquent or precise statement about the season: "Carnival is a butterfly of winter, whose last mad flight of Mardi Gras forever ends his glory. Another season is the glory of another butterfly, and the tattered, scattered, fragments of rainbow wings are in turn the record of his day."

Perry Young's contribution to local Carnival history is priceless. (Illustration by Arthur Nead)

Perry Swearingen Young was a journalist in New Orleans during the 1920s and '30s. He was a gifted writer who produced a local classic, *The Mistick Krewe: Chronicles of Comus and His Kin*—probably the most important book ever written about the origins of Carnival. All research about the season properly begins with a reading of this book.

Young was born in Abilene, Texas, not a likely beginning for someone who would receive a bachelor of arts degree from Yale and become a chronicler of New Orleans society. After graduating in 1909, he headed back to Texas, where he held maritime reporting jobs with the *Galveston Tribune* and the *Houston Post* before being drawn into World War I. After the war, he moved to New Orleans, where he inaugurated a magazine called *Gulf Ports*. Having established himself in this city, Young, in 1924, shifted to editing another port-related house organ, *World Port*, the monthly publication of the American Association of Port Authorities. Between then and 1933, he also opened his own business, Carnival Press, the name under which he wrote, edited, and published Carnival programs. *World Port* and Carnival Press operated out of the same office at 520 Whitney Bank Building, a spot that became the informal cradle of Carnival history.

There are many gaps in Young's story, but it might be supposed that in writing about ports and serving as the public-relations agent for the Dock Board, he rubbed shoulders with many of the city's prominent citizens, some of whom were part of the social side of Carnival. He belonged to Alexis, a very prominent social organization of the era, and was also invited to join the Pickwick Club. He wrote the programs for the Comus organization and might have belonged to it. His best offer came when the captain of Comus, Sylvester P. Walmsley, asked him to pen a history of the Mistick Krewe—the group that founded and maintained the New Orleans parading tradition. The book was to be prepared as a krewe gift to celebrate the group's seventy-fifth anniversary in 1932. It was a prize that even seemed worthy of press coverage, such as by *New Orleans States* columnist (and later congressman) F. Edward Hebert, who broke the news on Twelfth Night of that year that those in Comus's favor would receive the volume.

But then Young's career took a different turn. Walmsley had died, and the interim Comus captain had decided against the book. These were also hard times in the real world, as the glitter of Carnival was paled by the Great Depression. *World Port* magazine was moved to California, leaving its editor behind. Young maintained Carnival Press and also began publishing two other magazines, *Shore and Beach* and *Garden*. But the income was not steady.

His daughter, Zuma Young Salaun, once recalled to me that there was financial uneasiness during that time but her father was too proud to discuss his problems at home. "My mother wanted him to find a job like a streetcar driver," she remembered, "but he wasn't very mechanical; he would have wrecked the streetcar." Instead, the writer in him tried to prevail, churning out house organs and writing Carnival publications. Young was learned in the classics, mythology, and foreign languages, making him the right reporter to break through Carnival's lore with his book, *The Mistick Krewe: Chronicles of Comus and His Kin*. He wrote with a scholar's familiarity of the poet Ovid's description of the early pagan rites of spring. He collected engravings of early parades and listed those long forgotten who had worn the crowns. His was a record of New Orleans society written and presented in a style to embellish the grandest of reading-room coffee tables.

A first edition of The Mistick Krewe: Chronicles of Comus and His Kin. *(Courtesy of The Historic New Orleans Collection)*

Young died in 1939 at the age of fifty-one. Only about one thousand copies of his book had been distributed. In a warehouse, his daughter located approximately nine thousand unbound copies, from which she was able to distribute some of the engravings. Eventually, the remaining stock was sold for waste paper. Young was one of those writers who never fully knew his success. *The Mistick Krewe* remains timeless, although he died without reaping any profit from the book or likely realizing its importance.

In 1969, Zuma Young Salaun allowed the book to be reprinted. Having survived legal skirmishes with a publisher, Salaun claims to have regained control of the reprint, some copies of which were stacked in her closet. She had become a Carnival historian on her own, giving lectures, writing pamphlets, and remembering her father.

Perry Young was eulogized not so much as a historian but as an environmentalist. Of his writings in *Shore and Beach*, for example, it was said, "The cause of shore protection lost a valiant and gallant advocate . . . who did not strive for wealth." But Perry Young's memory has been preserved by Mardi

Gras, and he will be remembered each winter for his book that is so enriched by its opening lines.

Many seasons have passed since Perry Young completed *The Mistick Krewe*. Now there is a new generation of writers covering Carnival, any one of whom would be fortunate to one day look at the spectacle and see a butterfly.

CHAPTER 3

Free Spirits

HISTORIC WANDERINGS

Bare Facts about Showing It All

Disrobing, in various stages, during Carnival is not a New Orleans invention. Carnival traces back to pre-Christian times and a number of pre-spring rituals that included people romping naked in the fields. One of Carnival's ancestors, the Saturnalia, was celebrated with, among other traditions, a Roman orgy. The American Carnival, which after all was forged largely by Protestants, has always been fairly tame compared to its ancient origins and the contemporary Carnival in other places such as Rio, where dancers of both genders samba topless on the floats.

Members of the DIVAS, the Divine Protectors of Endangered Pleasures, wear corset-like costumes decorated with Mardi Gras beads. (Photo © Mitchel Osborne)

A view of a Carnival parade on Royal Street in the 1960s, as seen from the Rib Room Restaurant in the Royal Orleans Hotel. (Photo by Joe Budde)

Since the Vieux Carré has always had its naughty side, there has probably been some sort of nudity for as long as Carnival has been celebrated there. What is different in contemporary times, however, is that the spectacle has become more ritualized. There is now a titillating three-word chant suggesting which body part should be shown, and there is an easy-to-imagine counterpoint chant for females to direct at males. The chants are now sold on buttons and T-shirts and scribbled on signs.

I believe that the ritualized pleading traces back to when the parades were barred from the French Quarter in 1973. When the krewes marched through the Vieux Carré, they acted as a catharsis that moved and reshuffled the crowds. Without the krewes, the balconies became the new floats. People began throwing baubles back and forth, and one thing led to another. The chant, which has probably been yelled in various forms for as long as spring has been celebrated, was given permanence by technology that allows for just about anything to be printed on just about anything.

Someone asked me if there is more nudity in Carnival now than before. I am not sure. What there is certifiably more of is media, and that's the big difference. The word of what goes on in the Quarter isn't being spread so much by mainstream news organizations as by outlets that were once not available—the Internet (particularly YouTube) and self-made videos. People who create Web sites and videos look for niches. As the competition increases, so too must the niches multiply. Carnival bawdiness soon became one of them.

Those who are offended by stereotypes should skip this paragraph, as I suggest that the real offense to the senses is not the lewd exhibition itself but the fact that it tends to attract the species known as the college student. When totally lubricated, the male of that species is inclined to frequently emit a chilling primal yell that could drive tourists to Des Moines, even if they were not from there.

There is the issue of the image of Carnival and how it affects tourism. Carnival is still a family attraction, especially along St. Charles Avenue, where the floats roll beneath a canopy of oaks. Clamping down on the behavior in the Quarter would remove one element of what is perceived to be negative publicity. But positive publicity would not necessarily follow. More likely there would be no publicity at all. A pure, wholesome Carnival just doesn't make good copy (as the people in Las Vegas discovered when they realized the folly of their efforts to market the town as a family destination). In the age of Disney World and at a time when every community and hamlet is trying to develop a visitor industry, Carnival may level off as a tourist attraction. Try as we might to attract families, Carnival will never offer the controlled environment of a resort or amusement park. Even without the flesh, the tourist areas downtown during Carnival are, like all downtowns, inherently adult.

There will probably always be some show-me-something at Carnival, although the degree to which it is tolerated will more likely be regulated by the laws of economics than by city ordinance. How do I feel about the issue? I just want the parades back in the Quarter.

STORIES TOLD

Easy Riding

In 1969, the movie *Easy Rider* began its trek toward becoming a film classic. Stars Peter Fonda and Dennis Hopper ride motorcycles from California to New Orleans, both to experience the Mardi Gras and to discover the meaning of life

Opposite: *Mermaids from the DIVAS group on Mardi Gras Day.* (Photo © Mitchel Osborne)

Mardi gras night, Comus parade in the French Quarter — *Michael B. Smith, 1969*

The 1969 Comus parade coming down Royal Street, as captured by Michael P. Smith. As the size of some krewes' floats grew, safety concerns arose. City government banned Carnival parades in the French Quarter in 1973. (Courtesy of The Historic New Orleans Collection)

Comus parade in the French Quarter — *Michael P. Smith 1969*

Another view of the 1969 Comus parade in the French Quarter, photographed by Michael P. Smith. (Courtesy of The Historic New Orleans Collection)

A rare color photo of a nighttime parade in the French Quarter, as captured by photographer Jack Beech in 1967. (Courtesy of Joe Bergeron and New Orleans Magazine*)*

On Mardi Gras, French Quarter balconies are filled with revelers throwing beads to crowds. (Photo © Mitchel Osborne)

(which, of course, is easily found in New Orleans at Mardi Gras). In one famous scene, Fonda and Hopper, along with Jack Nicholson, whom they have picked up along the way, stop at a café, Melancon's, in the Pointe Coupee Parish town of Morganza. The threesome causes a stir among the townsfolk, who haven't seen much of their kind. A couple of rogue cops keep a suspicious eye on them and follow them to a spot along the river where they are camping out. That night, they are attacked and Nicholson is killed—thus was the conflict of the world's values played out, right there, near Morganza.

(Jack Nicholson, of course, would survive, to be seen frequently in later life sitting courtside at Los Angeles Lakers games. So much for class conflicts.)

Other Louisiana scenes for the movie were shot in the town of Franklin and in New Orleans, at Mardi Gras, as the search for meaning continued.

Some of that meaning was apparently found in St. Louis Cemetery No. 1, where the characters have a Mardi Gras afternoon romp with a couple of women. The scene is historic not only for the liberation that it suggests but also because of the subtle pounding in the background. In the distance can be seen the I-10 loop then under construction as it ravaged North Claiborne Avenue, that in itself a true symbol of social struggles.

Easy Rider created tension for the local Mardi Gras, as each year, for several Carnivals after, there would be rumors of hordes of flower children as well as bikers, including the Hell's Angels, heading to Mardi Gras. To this day some bikers do come, many parking their wheels at a designated spot on St. Peter Street, but they are searching for nothing more than a party.

For years after the film's release, Melancon's was a must-stop for devotees of the movie, and there were many. The lunch spot continued to operate as normal. Morganza never really took advantage of the fame that the film brought. Then, perhaps due to the completion of I-49, which bypassed it to the west, the café closed, and the building was eventually razed.

Highway building also had its impact on Carnival. That construction in the background while Fonda and Hopper romped in the cemetery would signal the end of the North Claiborne Avenue Mardi Gras celebration, an epicenter of Treme neighborhood activity. There, Mardi Gras Indians would walk the streets, masked groups such as the Skeletons and Baby Dolls would saunter along the block, and Zulu would reign. Singer Al Johnson recorded a song about a bar in the neighborhood that caught fire:

> The Green Room is smoking
> and the Plaza's burning down.
> Throw my baby out the window
> and let the joint burn down.
> All because it's Carnival time.

One day, demolition crews would arrive, and the neighborhood's fate would be worse than a fire.

In Morganza, where the film was gradually accepted for historic value though long shunned because of its portrayal of the community, there is now a marker commemorating *Easy Rider* in the sidewalk in front of the empty lot where Melancon's once stood. The town today is as quiet as ever. Something else that hasn't changed: beware of the cops, not for brutality but for chasing automobiles whose drivers do not heed the speed-limit signs. In the town where Peter Fonda and Dennis Hopper once searched for peace, traffic tickets are an economic stimulus.

The bikers were looking for the meaning of life. In doing so, they, and all of us, learned the wisdom in heeding the signs along the way. Nevertheless, the free spirit still beckons.

CHAPTER 4

The Ladies

HISTORIC WANDERINGS

March of the Queens

Although most of Rex's queens have had elegant names that often reflect old-family connections, let it be noted that the very first queen of Carnival was named Fanny.

Mrs. Walker Fearn attended the 1873 Rex Ball, little knowing she would be selected as the queen of Carnival. Of course, if she had known, she later lamented, she would have worn a more formal gown. The scene is depicted in artist George Schmidt's Mrs Walker Fearn Being Made the First Queen of Carnival, 1873. *(Courtesy of George Schmidt)*

In 1872, Rex staged its first parade. A year later, the king's first Carnival ball was held. At that ball, the reigning Rex, E. B. Wheelock, selected a woman from the audience to be his queen. History, and the society notes, would record her as being Mrs. Walker Fearn. Her maiden name was Fanny Hewitt. The debutante tradition had not begun yet, so the first queen was the only married woman to have sat on the throne.

Little has been known about that queen or her husband. Recent research, however, has shown the Fearns to be a couple that certainly reflected the elegance and the turmoil of the time. Just as the first Rex, Lewis Salomon, was from Mobile, so was the husband of the first queen. Walker Fearn, a lawyer who had served as a diplomat to Belgium during the James Buchanan administration, was well known in New Orleans. His mother was a prominent socialite in Mobile.

Little is known about Fanny Hewitt other than that Fearn met her while he was serving in the Confederate military in Texas. Thus, the first queen of Carnival was a war bride. That her reign was unexpected was made apparent by her one complaint about the honor: she hadn't worn her best dress that evening.

As the debutante tradition became a part of Carnival balls, the nature of those

Debutantes are presented during the New Orleans Carnival season. Shown, Caroline Somerville Nead, with her father, Arthur Nead. (Photo by Peggy Scott Laborde)

who were honored changed. Rex's queens would be unmarried; socially well connected; juniors in college; and clearly wearing their best dresses, ones created especially for the occasion. Months of preparation and partying go into the reign, and the selection is hardly spontaneous. Some girls have been groomed to serve on a future court practically from birth.

A lot of preparation is required for a one-day reign, although often overlooked, even by the girls themselves, is the fact that queens play a role that is enduring. Because they are far younger than their reigning Rexes, queens often provide the longest-lasting memories of the big day and the enchanted night. Fanny Hewitt Fearn had a one-night shot at immortality. Hers was a Cinderella ride. Even a second-best dress looks better when embellished by a crown.

Like real royalty, Carnival royalty is occasionally vulnerable to cheap shots from the national press. In 2001, an article in the *New York Times Magazine* used unflattering photos and an ignorant headline, "Cajun Cotillion," to poke fun at the tradition, although the article itself paid more deference. Teasing comes easily; more intellectually challenging is trying to understand the debutante tradition, which at its primal level is as innocent as a proud father honoring his daughter. At a more complex level, such traditions involve old-family lineages and customs and are quite healthy for a community if they give the families incentive to remain a part of it. Every town should have traditions that offer its people a limousine night, if only once in a lifetime.

Some of the best of the *Times* article centered on comments from debutante Blayne Laborde and her mother, Peggy (no relation). That previous Carnival season, Blayne, then an architecture major at the University of Virginia, ruled as queen of the high-society Osiris organization and served as a maid in the courts of Rex, Proteus, and Mithras. The article quoted Blayne as saying her reign was "much more fun than I thought it would be; I honestly felt like a queen."

Mom Peggy put it all in perspective by offering a quote that should be required reading for anyone who wants to write another article about New Orleans debutantes: "It's just a fun thing to do. These girls are very bright and focused individuals."

Even more in keeping with the spirit of the modern debutante is the story told to me by Mary Louise "M. L." Phelps, who in 1999 was the queen of Carnival on the same day that her cousin, Muffin Labouisse, was the Comus queen. After the ball was the Queens Supper, which lasted until around 2:00 A.M. Following that, they still had their dates to accompany them and a limousine for their use. They went home and changed and then, wearing jeans and their crowns, partied at the F&M Patio Bar on Tchoupitoulas Street until sunrise. Jeans and a crown—that's the American debutante experience.

STORIES TOLD

Inspiration Tickles the Muse

People have been known to find inspiration from spiritual leaders, though seldom in modern times has motivation come from Druids. Yet that happened in 2000 to an attorney named Staci Rosenberg, and the inspiration tickled the muse within her. "I was inspired to start Muses by Druids, although I'm not sure whether they know that," Rosenberg wrote me. "A lawyer in my office rode in Druids, and I had been out watching the parade and thinking about how much fun everyone seemed to be having. I realized that I would love to be in a parade, but I couldn't think of an existing one that I thought would be a good fit. As soon as I got home, I called Weezie Porter and said, 'If I start a Mardi Gras parade, do you want to be in it?' For some reason I said, 'Let's make it just for women.' Very matter-of-factly, Weezie said: 'Sure, I'll be in it. Hold on, I have some people here; let's see if they want to be in it, too.' They all wanted to, and a few months later, Muses was born!"

Inspiration that night had come from the krewe known officially as the Mystic Krewe of Druids, which itself was an upstart, being formed in 1998 by Carnival insiders as a way of giving other krewe organizers a worry-free way to experience a parade.

Muses would not be just another parade. It would rock Mardi Gras. There had been all-female krewes before but not one founded in an age when women were so much a part of the professional workforce and not one that would deliver its message with satire and not one that would invite so many marching groups to join its ranks. The new krewe would open the door to Carnival, letting even more people in. The parade made its debut during the 2001 Carnival season.

The Muff-A-Lottas dance troupe performs in the Muses parade. (Photo © Judi Bottoni)

The Krewe of Muses is an all-women's group that parades on the Thursday evening before Carnival. Its symbol is a woman's shoe, and krewe members give out decorated shoes as throws. (Photo © Mitchel Osborne)

The Pussyfooters are among the many marching groups that parade in Muses. (Photo © Mitchel Osborne)

The Camel Toe Lady Steppers, in their vibrant pink costumes and feathers, march in the Muses parade each year. (Photo © Mitchel Osborne)

Muses floats use cartoon-like murals to convey the parade's satirical theme. While most are humorous, after Katrina this float summed up the feeling of many New Orleans residents. (Photo © Mitchel Osborne)

The Lady Godiva Riding Club wears nude-colored bodysuits. They are a fixture in the Muses parade. (Photo © Mitchel Osborne)

The Bearded Oysters is one of many small groups that march in the Muses parade. (Photo © Mitchel Osborne)

The Muses parade and many others feature high-school drill teams.
(Photo © Mitchel Osborne)

"There were fewer obstacles in starting the organization than one might expect," Rosenberg said, "mainly because we had no idea what was involved and we didn't really notice the obstacles at the time. Our biggest challenge was getting an ordinance introduced to have Muses added to the parade calendar. We had a number of city employees as early members and found the Council members to be generally supportive."

According to Rosenberg, one perceived obstacle actually worked to the fledgling krewe's advantage. "No one in the Mardi Gras community thought we would succeed. But this became an advantage also since it led to the Kerns [float builders] charging us very little since they thought we couldn't afford it and we would fail. It was also hard to get bands because it was a weeknight and they had never heard of us and thought they wouldn't get paid. We were definitely the blind leading the blind, but it seemed to work out."

The entry into Carnival of Kristin Danflous, who in 2011 at age thirty-two became captain of the Krewe of Iris, the oldest surviving female parading organization, was not spontaneous but more or less inherited. "I have been involved in Iris since I was a small child; I was a page for seven years," she wrote me. "My grandmother Joy Oswald was captain for twenty-four years before me, and her aunt and my great-aunt [Irma Strode] was captain thirty-two years before her. So I guess it is in my blood."

Having taken over a long-established krewe, the greatest challenges for her are operational, including coordination with the costume makers, the float builders, and "the companies overseas manufacturing our throws."

Kristin Danflous, the current captain of the Krewe of Iris, is a relative of former longtime captain Irma Strode. (Photo by Peggy Scott Laborde)

"Our krewe members aren't thinking about Mardi Gras in the middle of summer so getting them excited and ready to pay their dues so we can pay for floats, costumes for 900 members, bands, and have everything completed by early February is a challenge," she said.

Then there are the elements. "The toughest thing I have had to do as captain is reschedule the parade due to severe weather threats. I would not wish that on anyone. It takes an entire year to plan a parade and to have to realign each piece of the massive puzzle was the biggest obstacle to overcome."

"What I like most about being captain," she added, "is when I see the members' faces as they get off the float and they are smiling and telling stories of their ride. And you hear words like 'I had the time of my life' or 'I can't wait until next year' or—my favorite—'I got to get my sister to ride next year! I had a blast!' Then I get the members that come up to me and give me a big hug and say: 'You are doing a great job. Thanks for everything.' I say, 'You are so welcome' and give them a smile, and I think to myself: 'Just wait until next year! Iris is bloomin'!!!' How can you not like that?"

Favorite Stories

A Little Girl's Vision, by Staci Rosenberg

When Muses was eleven years old, the eleven-year-old daughter of a lawyer in my

Irma Strode, left, was captain of the Krewe of Iris for over thirty years.
(Photo © Mitchel Osborne)

office was visiting on a Saturday. When I saw her, she ran over and said, "Me and my friends were talking, and we thought if there was ever a parade just for boys, it should be called Mooses." I love this story because this little girl did not even realize that there were any parades "just for boys," but for her entire existence she knew there had been a parade just for girls. I also love that she wanted to call boys mooses!

Becoming Captain, by Kristin Danflous

The story that sticks out in my mind the most is when my grandmother passed the fan to me at the ball. It was my rite of passage; it was a huge emu-feathered fan that was encrusted in rhinestones. I remember it like it was yesterday, I was standing behind the curtain, and I could hear the announcer giving the history of my family and hear him say, "Now for only the second time in fifty years, this fan will be passed to your new captain!" And the curtains opened, and the ballroom filled with smoke, and then I heard "One" [the song from A Chorus Line] played, and I walked out in my royal-blue dress with my white emu fan, and I greeted my krewe. That moment was a moment I will never forget!

A rider in the Iris parade. (Photo © Mitchel Osborne)

The all-female Iris parade, which debuted in the 1950s, traditionally rolls on the Saturday before Mardi Gras. (Photo © Mitchel Osborne)

The Baby Dolls, a longtime tradition in the New Orleans black community, feature women dressed as dolls. Once virtually extinct, the tradition is experiencing a revival. This Baby Doll is shown marching in the Muses parade. (Photo © Mitchel Osborne)

CHAPTER 5

Captains

HISTORIC WANDERINGS

Important Job, No Recognition

In the final hour of Carnival 2002, a rare but important ritual was enacted—and hardly anyone noticed. The ceremony was also one of Carnival's briefest. As the Rex Ball was closing—after the king and queen had left their thrones and while most from the audience were either heading home or moving to the Comus Ball—two men in white ties and tails approached each other from different points on the floor. The men's meeting point was in front of the box seats where both of their wives happened to be. Reaching their destination, the two stood face to face. Then something happened that elicited gasps from those few left in the auditorium who happened to be watching. One of the men lifted his whistle cord from around his neck and placed it around the neck of the other. There were applause, a few cheers, and lots of expressions of surprise. The queen of Carnival, who happened to be looking back at the ball floor on her way to meet Comus, seemed tearful, happy, and astonished. The man who received the whistle was her dad.

For a celebration that thrives on pageantry, one of its most important transitions happens simply. The passing of the whistle signaled a change in the captaincy of the Rex organization.

Tradition has it that the identity of the Rex captain is kept secret. The reason for that, as Mark Twain once wrote in explaining the rituals of the local Carnival, is not for fear of the police but for the sake of tradition itself. In the power structure of Carnival, the captains are the bosses of their krewes. While the reign of monarchs lasts just for a day and their duties are strictly ceremonial, captains act as prime ministers, concerned with day-to-day governance.

Although every krewe has a captain, the man who wears the whistle for Rex historically takes on the extra responsibility of guiding all of Carnival. "It is the best civic job there is," the then-outgoing captain used to say about the position he held for nearly nine years. If so, it is *not* because of political or business gains that might come with the title. Secret jobs are hardly factors in career advancement. Besides, the men who become captain have usually already found their places in the corporate world. Other than getting to ride a white horse and being invited to lots of debutante parties, few perks come with the job. But for those who like to mix it up with everyday issues and controversies, atop

The captain of Rex wears the traditional gold costume for the parade. (Photo © Mitchel Osborne)

The captain of Endymion on his float adorned with a fleur de-lis, a symbol of New Orleans.
(Photo © Mitchel Osborne)

The captain of Proteus greets the author along the parade route during the early 1990s. (Photo by Peggy Scott Laborde)

The captain of Babylon visits with a tiny parade-goer. (Photo © Mitchel Osborne)

the white horse is the place to be. Whenever Carnival has had crises, Rex's captains have usually been up front facing them. In 1979, when a police strike caused all parades in New Orleans to be canceled, the Rex captain of that time stood alongside Mayor Ernest "Dutch" Morial in defying the union organizers. During the anti-discrimination ordinance controversy of 1991-92, a different Rex captain stood courageously in front of the New Orleans City Council taking the heat from both sides: some fellow captains who thought he was being too accommodating versus the ordinance's proponents who thought he was not being accommodating enough. The captain also worked behind the scenes to bring about the relatively peaceful resolution of the crisis, largely due to legal problem-solving initiated by Rex leadership.

One recent Rex captain served as chairman of the city's Mardi Gras Coordinating Committee, having to deal with issues ranging from the mundane—float fire-extinguisher specifications—to the critical—Carnival safety hazards.

The Rex organization's first captain was E. C. Hancock, a newspaperman with a flair for the literary. Even in its founding, Rex was solving a problem by creating a day parade that would attract more tourists to the city, during the tense years of Reconstruction when people were nervous about traveling here. By claiming the title of King of Carnival, the group also created a populist monarch.

As Carnival grew and other krewes were founded, Rex, by the mid-twentieth century, had fallen into the shadows—still parading but without much sparkle. By the early 1960s, however, a Rex revival was taking place under the leadership of the late Darwin Fenner, who is credited with rebuilding the organization.

In the age of the superkrewe, Rex is neither the biggest nor the richest of the parading organizations, but it is the group with the best grasp of Carnival's traditions, style, and elegance. As holder of the title "King of Carnival," Rex takes its civic responsibilities seriously.

Among the traditions for most krewes, including Rex, is that the captaincy is an unpaid position. The significance of that became evident in the summer of 2012, when one of the superkrewes faced a steep dues increase. Comparative data leaked over the Internet showed that krewe's captain's son received a six-figure salary as a director, while for Rex and most others, the dollar figure for salary and travel was zero.

At the end of the 2011 Rex Ball, two men dressed in white ties and tails approached each other, and once more the whistle changed hands. I have never been one to define Carnival's significance in terms of economic impact alone. The season also fosters community spirit and provides an urban identity. When Mardi Gras is measured in terms of tourism dollars, however, those who are its leaders are as civically important as the forces behind the Jazz Fest and the Convention Center, except the Carnival guys wear masks.

One also wears a whistle. When thunder is heard during Carnival, sometimes

it's from gathering storm clouds and sometimes it is just approaching drums. While others revel, the man on the white horse has to be ready to respond to either situation.

STORIES TOLD

A Captain's Legacy

He was not among Comus's founders, but Albert Walter Merriam would become a towering figure in the organization. Merriam, one of several young men invited to join after the first parade, was born in 1826 in Ware, Massachusetts. He would eventually become captain of Comus, serving from 1872 to 1874. Merriam's first year as captain was pivotal in the evolution of New Orleans' Carnival celebration, for in that year the Rex organization was founded. As captain of Comus, Merriam had a hand in starting Rex, as did other Comus members. Rex would give Carnival a daytime parade, expand participation in Carnival, and give the season a public persona as opposed to the more secretive Comus.

Among all the businesses of Carnival's founders, Merriam's was easily the most popular and the most visible. In 1865, Merriam bought the building on the corner of Canal Street and St. Charles Street that before the Civil War had been the Merchants' Hotel and that during the war had been taken over to house federal troops. Merriam combined the two upper stories to make an elegant billiard hall known as Crescent Hall, which would become an important gathering place for the overwhelmingly male downtown workforce. Then, for a whopping $5,000, he added a veranda that was eighteen feet wide on Canal Street and sixteen feet on St. Charles. The first floor was laid with mosaic tiles and housed various shops, including purveyors of wines and cigars and an oyster house.

The Rex organization was founded a block away in the St. Charles Hotel, but one can imagine plans of upcoming parades and the details of Rex being discussed over billiards at the Crescent Hall. The building's place in male society would survive; it eventually became the home of the Pickwick Club, as it still is today. It would be on Merriam's galleries that the Comus courts of the future would watch the parades march by.

During Merriam's three years as captain, Comus staged one of Carnival's all-time most controversial parades. The 1873 march was a political satire that poked fun at the federal occupiers during those tense days of Reconstruction. Titled "Missing Links to Darwin's *Origin of the Species*," the parade depicted various occupiers as animals, including Gen. Benjamin Butler, the head of the local federal forces, who was shown as a hyena, and cigar-smoking Pres. Ulysses S. Grant, who was represented as a tobacco grub. The parade triggered a flurry of telegrams between New Orleans and Washington in an attempt to cool tempers. Charles Darwin himself was sent a copy of Comus's souvenir program and a newspaper article attacking his theories. He responded, "The abusive article in the newspaper amused me more than Comus."

On Mardi Gras night in 1874, Merriam, as captain, led the Comus parade. When he reached Crescent Hall at Canal and St. Charles, he left the parade so

Opposite: *The captain of Druids wearing a traditional tri-plumed hat.* (Photo © Mitchel Osborne)

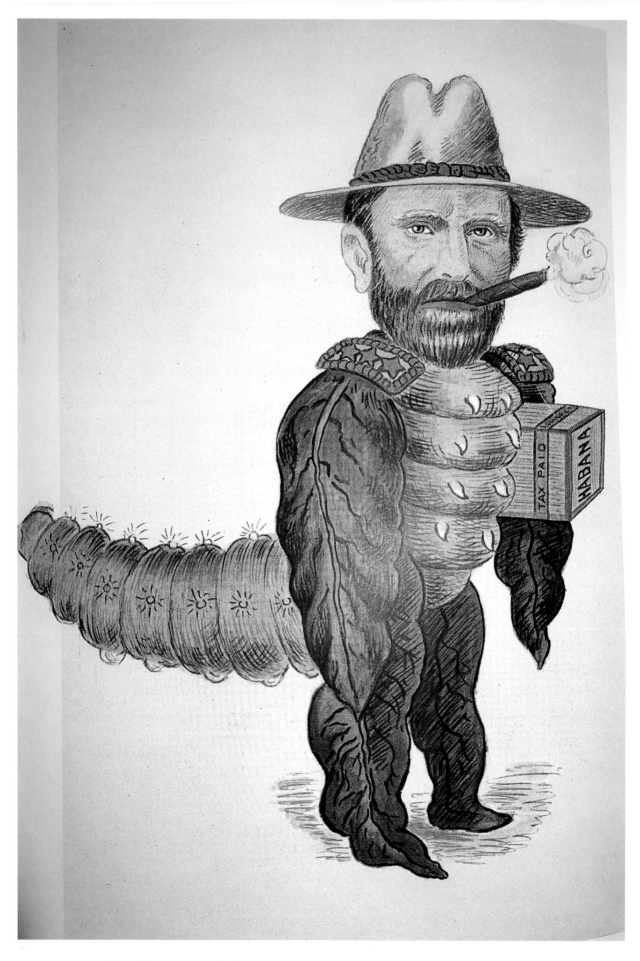

The 1873 Comus parade skewered the cigar-smoking President Grant, depicting him as a tobacco grub. The theme was titled "Missing Links to Darwin's Origin of Species." (From The Mistick Krewe: Chronicles of Comus and His Kin, by Perry Young)

that he could review the procession from the gallery. He saluted each float as it passed by.

After the parade, Merriam went to the Varieties Theatre for the Comus tableaux and then attended the post-ball supper. Then he entertained some friends at home until he retired around 3:00 A.M. Within a few hours Merriam suffered a stroke, collapsed, and never regained consciousness. On the afternoon after Mardi Gras, less than twenty-four hours after he led Comus, his funeral was held at his home at 587 St. Charles.

A resolution from the Pickwick Club published in a newspaper bemoaned the loss, saying that he "leaves to us the heritage of his virtues and his goodness."

Albert Walter Merriam would be among the first of many Carnival organizers who lived for Mardi Gras.

Parallel Lives: Three Captains Speak

The Trojan horse is a signature float of the Krewe of Orpheus. (Photo © Mitchel Osborne)

A rare view of the captain of Sparta preparing his parade as it forms along Napoleon Avenue. He will shortly don his captain's plumed hat. (Photo by Errol Laborde)

By tradition, in many krewes the identities of the captains remain secret, though that is not so in the superkrewes. Here are comments from the captains of two of the traditionally secretive krewes as well as Sonny Borey, a longtime theater director who is the founding captain of superkrewe Orpheus.

How did you become captain?

Le Krewe d'Etat captain: I was selected by a nominating committee and approved by the board of directors. That is the way our organization does it. You do not apply or ask; you are asked. That is the traditional way of choosing a captain.

Orpheus captain: Harry Connick, Jr., was Bacchus for their twenty-fifth-anniversary parade. He had a great time but was also concerned about the fallout from the Dorothy Mae Taylor [anti-discrimination] ordinance. He wanted a krewe that was open to all of good character. He also wanted a continuation of the weekend that would keep tourists in the city through Tuesday. He called, we got together—and the rest is history.

Sparta captain: I was an officer in the Knights of Sparta for over twenty-five years, all during the tenure of the late Charles Andrews as captain. I was, of course, very involved, and when he decided to retire as captain in 2005, I was elected captain. I am only the third captain in the sixty-one-year history of Sparta. Our captain is basically elected "captain for life."

What do you like most about the job?

Le Krewe d'Etat captain: The thing I enjoy most is organizing, planning, and putting on the parade—things like choosing and developing a theme. I also enjoy working with the many great members who are part of organizing and planning the parade.

Orpheus captain: The theatrical aspect . . . it is a theater production on the streets of our city. And you know my deep love for musical theater and pageantry. That love and parades are a great fit.

Sparta captain: I love all of the behind-the-scenes work (writing the Bal Masque script; working with the costumer; working with the court; selecting the music; working with scenic effects, lighting, actors, singers, dancers, etc., for the ball; working with float themes for the parade and with the float builder, etc.).

What do you like least?

Le Krewe d'Etat captain: Choosing who our pages are going to be. We only have four spots and get twelve to fifteen or more requests per year. I don't like to disappoint members and their families. That and I also don't like to have to discipline or expel members.

Orpheus captain: Absolutely nothing. I love it, but the amount of hours is staggering—it's like directing and producing three musicals at the same time. I especially like the planning in the months that lead up to Orpheus Monday. The parade itself gives me the most worry moments—in a way that makes sense: I have always felt the same watching one of my productions.

Sparta captain: Making sure that all of our members follow our rules and traditions. We do not tolerate unmasked riders, inebriated riders, lewd throws, etc. The vast majority of our members adhere strictly to our rules; however, when a few try to test the limits of noncompliance, the captain must step in and read them the riot act. I would much rather not have to do that. Several years ago I [and the officers] had to expel three full floats of riders for rule-breaking. It was not an easy thing to do, especially in this economy, but we felt that we had to maintain our traditions, and I am happy to say that we replaced them within a year and actually rode with a larger krewe membership the next year.

Do you have a favorite memory or anecdote?

Le Krewe d'Etat captain: A couple things come to mind. My first parade when we turned from Napoleon Avenue onto St. Charles, and there was this sea of humanity cheering. That was a thrill. The anecdote would be the year we had a flambeau carrier get arrested during the parade and give the flambeau to a relative who was nearby who then returned it to the krewe in order to get the money he was to be paid to carry the flambeau in the parade.

Orpheus captain: There are many: watching the people at the Orpheuscapade go wild when Harry performed with Stevie Wonder, Vanessa Williams, Brad Paisley, James Brown, and Branford Marsalis to name a few; seeing the crowd applaud as the Leviathan [float] rolled down the street for the first time and not asking for beads; the comments from the crowd about the flowers that cover our floats. Each parade is special for me, but oh, how privileged I feel to be a part of New Orleans Mardi Gras history!

Sparta captain: I became captain in May of 2005 and was really looking forward to my first year. Of course, Katrina hit in August, and we were not sure if Mardi Gras would even be held in 2006. The venues for our coronation and Bal Masque were damaged, and I decided to hold back on staging a coronation and Bal Masque and allow my court to be "held over" until the next season. However, as you know, after much work with the city, we were able to stage our parade (albeit a combined parade of all of the first weekend's parades). We were able to amass seven floats of members, and, as is our tradition, the captain and officers led our part of the parade on horseback. That first ride up St. Charles Avenue on a white horse leading our parade was one that I will never forget. I tell everyone that I really did not ride the horse—because I was riding about two feet above the saddle. It was then that I really knew that Mardi Gras—and Sparta—were back to stay.

CHAPTER 6

Louisiana Carnival

HISTORIC WANDERINGS

The Three Strains of Carnival in Louisiana

At its simplest, Carnival is folks standing on curbs catching beads. But if one looks closer, Carnival is a season with deep cultural roots. Examine Carnival in Louisiana, and you will see a celebration with three distinct identities. Here are some questions and answers.

Straw finger pulls and glass beads from either Czechoslovakia or Japan were popular throws in the 1950s and '60s. (From the collection of Peggy Scott Laborde)

79

The captain's float in the Caesar parade in Jefferson Parish. This krewe is known for its elaborate costumes. (Photo © Mitchel Osborne)

A maid in the Caesar parade wears a detailed headdress. (Photo © Mitchel Osborne)

This parking sign from the 1960s was used to denote a parade route. (From the collection of Peggy Scott Laborde)

A 1970 scene in Mamou, Louisiana, of participants engaging in the Courir de Mardi Gras. Translated as "Fat Tuesday Run," this tradition includes visits to local homes begging for chickens and other ingredients for a gumbo. (Courtesy of the Louisiana Division/City Archives, New Orleans Public Library)

What are the three strains of Carnival in Louisiana?

One is the New Orleans-style Carnival, which is by far the largest; another is the Acadian Courir de Mardi Gras; and the third is the Mardi Gras Indian tradition.

What are the characteristics of the New Orleans-style Carnival?

Just about everywhere in the state, or the continent, where there is a Mardi Gras celebration, it borrows from the New Orleans style. Characteristics would include floats with masked riders throwing trinkets; king cakes; the use of the colors purple, green, and gold; use of the term "krewe"; and organizations having kings or queens. All those are influenced by the Mardi Gras celebration that evolved in New Orleans.

Where, outside the New Orleans area, are New Orleans-style Carnivals held in Louisiana?

Some of the older celebrations are in Shreveport and New Roads. Baton Rouge, Lafayette, and—increasingly—Lake Charles have also developed a parade scene, as have many smaller towns including Bogalusa. In some places, however, the parades are on the weekend before Mardi Gras rather than the Tuesday itself. Of course, anyplace where king cakes are cut borrows from New Orleans.

Is there a difference in the way New Orleans-style Carnivals are celebrated outside of New Orleans?

In many areas, the "krewes" are really social-service organizations, quite often using their parades as fundraisers. Some areas are more lax in the quality of masking and the originality of float building. Common to most of them, though, is throwing items from floats.

What are the characteristics of the Cajun Courir de Mardi Gras?

Through the centuries there have been many examples of "visitation" traditions as a form of celebration—and not just at Carnival time. The early Mummers in Philadelphia, for example, would wear costumes and visit from house to house on New Year's Day. Courir de Mardi Gras is a visitation tradition in that masked horseback riders, often followed by a bandwagon, make their "run" (*courir*) by going from house to house to "beg" for ingredients for a gumbo.

Where is the Courir celebrated?

In Cajun Country, particularly west of the Atchafalaya in the Cajun prairie area around Mamou and Eunice.

What are the roots of those two Carnivals?

Although "Mardi Gras" is a French name and New Orleans was a French town, the Carnival that evolved there was largely Anglo-Saxon in influence (including the creation of the word "krewe"). With lineage that traces back to Mobile and farther back to the Mummers in Philadelphia, what evolved in New Orleans is the classic American Carnival, which, like many things American, has a touch of European influence. The

Capuchons, cone-style hats, are often a part of the costuming tradition in the Courir de Mardi Gras, held in many of the Cajun communities in southwestern Louisiana. This 2011 photo was taken in Savoy, Louisiana. (Photo by Herb Roe)

A child's first Mardi Gras. (Photo by Peggy Scott Laborde)

Opposite: *A tiny masker on Mardi Gras Day.* (Photo © Mitchel Osborne)

Courir's roots trace more directly back to medieval France.

How do the Mummers tie in to Carnival in Mobile and New Orleans?

Evidence shows that the Mummers influenced those who founded the Mobile Mardi Gras. (Indeed, the leader was from near Philadelphia.) The Mobile group was known as the Cowbellians, and in their initial march, on New Year's Day 1831, they made stops, including at the home of the mayor, so there was a trace of the Mummer visitation tradition. Years later, in 1857, some former Mobile Cowbellians would be instrumental in founding the Mistick Krewe of Comus in New Orleans. Besides creating the word "krewe" and introducing the float to the New Orleans Carnival, Comus would originate the city's parading tradition, from which all else evolved. Early Philadelphia Mummery was a distant influence on what evolved in New Orleans, yet, because of its European roots (primarily Scandinavian), Mummery also had characteristics of the celebration held in Cajun Country.

What are the roots of the Mardi Gras Indian tradition?

This third strain of Carnival in Louisiana is celebrated mostly among black males in New Orleans and fuses American Indian culture with Afro-Caribbean rhythms. The feathery Indian costumes borrow not from the local Choctaws but from American Plains Indians.

What is the traditional music of these three Carnivals?

Each has made rich contributions to Louisiana music. In New Orleans, there are mostly rhythm-and-blues standards (the classic being "Go to the Mardi Gras," sung by Bogalusa native Professor Longhair), and in Acadiana there are, of course, Cajun songs, with the anthem being "La Chanson de Mardi Gras." The Mardi Gras Indians' chants combine R&B with a Caribbean beat, the best-known example being "Iko, Iko."

Are the various Carnival strains influenced by geography and race?

Not necessarily. For example, although Lafayette is the epicenter of Cajun Country, the parades held there are more in keeping with the traditional New Orleans style. In New Orleans, the predominantly black Zulu parade is also more in keeping with the New Orleans style and not with the Mardi Gras Indian tradition.

Does any other state have so many different strains of Carnival?

No, most are usually a watered-down knockoff of the New Orleans version, with no real history.

What does all this prove?

It proves what a culturally rich state Louisiana is.

Musicians gather at a 2010 Courir de Mardi Gras. (Photo by Herb Roe)

Opposite: *The Mardi Gras Indian tradition is a fusion of Afro-Caribbean culture and American Indian culture.* (Photo © Mitchel Osborne)

While Mardi Gras Indians are most often seen on Carnival Day, some make special appearances on a Sunday near St. Joseph's Day (March 19). Some tribes also appear at the New Orleans Jazz and Heritage Festival. (Photo © Mitchel Osborne)

The Mardi Gras Indians sew their own intricately designed costumes. (Photo © Mitchel Osborne)

STORIES TOLD

Reigning in Imperial Calcasieu

As our carriage drew up to the building that houses the Mardi Gras Museum of Imperial Calcasieu in Lake Charles, a group of masked revelers was waiting in the parking lot. When the mule stopped, the revelers approached us and began tossing beads, while someone toted a boom box blasting Carnival music.

Our tour group had just been taken for a ride through Lake Charles' Charpentier District, an area of distinctive older house built back in the days when there were few architects but many creative carpenters (*charpentiers*), who often designed the houses on a whim. At the end of our ride stood a converted school that now serves as an arts and humanities center, part of which includes the Mardi Gras Museum of Imperial Calcasieu. Mardi Gras? Lake Charles? A museum?

Lake Charles has always been a culturally perplexing town. Located a little too far east of the border to be totally Texan in character and a little too far west of the Atchafalaya to be totally Cajun, it is a hybrid blended with other American elements. Interstate 10 has brought them all here, including the Louisiana Carnival as it has moved west from New Orleans.

A giant king cake baby greets visitors at the Mardi Gras Museum of Imperial Calcasieu. (Photo by Peggy Scott Laborde)

Mardi Gras as it developed in New Orleans runs historically and sociologically deep, borrowing elements from eastern American and European traditions and with some parts linked to the city's social scene. As the celebration spreads from New Orleans, however, the complexity decreases considerably. Carnival in other places is celebrated as an anticipated tourism boomlet, most often with some charitable connections and frequently sold as being family friendly. At its simplest, other towns want to party, too.

Lake Charles has not only embraced the Mardi Gras but also positioned itself as the celebration's capital in Southwest Louisiana. The museum serves as its archive, holding what is billed as "the largest collection of Mardi Gras costumes on the Gulf Coast." If someone knew absolutely nothing about the Louisiana Carnival celebration and spent a day in the museum, which even includes a robotic king cake baby explaining the king cake tradition, he or she will have mastered advanced studies on the subject.

Carnival as it is celebrated in Louisiana borrows much from New Orleans, but then, as happens in evolution, it takes on a character of its own. There are elements of the New Orleans Carnival at its best, including quality float-making and original costuming for float riders, while other elements fall short yet maintain their own feel. As the homes in the Charpentier District prove, for something to become enduring, it may not need a master plan, but imagination and quality will keep it on the map.

Having a Ball in Washington

Carnival's palace in New Orleans is whatever ballroom where, in the waning hours of the season, Rex bows to Comus. But in the eastern province of Carnival's American empire stands another palace, known to the unknowing merely as the Washington Hilton Hotel. Below the hotel's lobby exists a ballroom that ranks as one of the District's largest meeting spaces. Every inch is used to contain the annual Saturday-night soiree of the Mystick Krewe of Louisianians. By the time I got to Washington that afternoon in 2003, many ball-goers already seemed tired from two days of parties hosted by politicians, special-interest groups, and miscellaneous businesses. That night, we fresh arrivals at least brought clear vision and sober expectations to the ball.

In an opening ceremony, krewe officers, who that year were dressed like characters from the Louisiana Purchase, bowed from the stage, and the king and queen were introduced. Then came the presentation of a line of maids, each one representing a Louisiana festival, that could have stretched to Baltimore. A parade of mini-floats followed, serpentining through the ballroom. There was a float for each of the state's members of Congress and, on foot, a corresponding masked entourage, who tossed trinkets to the waving, ball-gloved hands. The procession included many politicians, though no one could be certain who was who because they were all masked.

Towering Carnival figures decorated the ballroom, hotel lobby, and even the building's front entrance. Among my surprises was learning that the ball was such a big production. To deliver the props and mini-floats, New Orleans float builder Blaine Kern had hired four eighteen-wheeler trucks.

Each member of the Louisiana congressional delegation has his or her own marching club at the Mystick Krewe of Louisianians Ball. (Photo by George Long)

Since the mid-1940s, members of the Louisiana congressional delegation and some local businessmen have staged a Mardi Gras ball in the nation's capital. In this scene from 2012, note the queen's elaborate mantle, which featured a pelican, the state bird, at the bottom. (Photo by George Long)

Another surprise was that after three days of festivities, the parties continued after the ball, even before the dancing in the main room was done. Down a hall, the Jefferson Parish Chamber of Commerce threw a Samba Soiree where rum drinks flowed and a samba band led a conga line through the crowd. In another meeting room, a krewe member hosted a private breakfast. Throughout the halls, would-be candidates for the then-upcoming state elections hoped for that fateful encounter that would fuel their bandwagon.

Activities continued, so the transition from night to sunrise was fuzzy. Later that next morning, sprawled throughout the lobby of the Washington Hilton, were the young women, now dressed in sandals and jeans, who the night before had glowed as maids. They were going home in the same way they got there, on a chartered jet—now taking them nonstop to Baton Rouge.

"You're from Louisiana," a taxi driver told me without having to ask. The law of probability was on his side. According to New Orleans businessman Joe Rault, a high-ranking official of the krewe, 70 percent of the 3,000 ball attendees were from the state. They packed not only the Washington Hilton but also the two hotels across the street. (The room where the ball is held is so big that, at the 2011 ball, the bands from Southern University and Grambling University competed in a battle of the bands, with each group stationed at an end of the hall, and there was still plenty of space in between.)

By Sunday evening, most of the Louisianians were heading home, where the Mardi Gras celebrations were just beginning.

HISTORY IN THE BALLROOM

A less festive part of the Washington Hilton's history is the fact that, in 1981, Pres. Ronald Reagan was shot on the way to his limousine after making a speech in its ballroom. The area of the incident has since been converted into a protected entranceway. The evening of the 2003 ball would also be marred by a historic tragedy. Earlier that day, the space shuttle *Columbia* had exploded during its reentry. The ball's opening program was revised to include a prayer and a moment of silence.

Another historic footnote took place on May 1, 2011. The two biggest events staged in the ballroom each year are the Louisiana Mardi Gras ball and the White House Correspondents Dinner. It was there that Pres. Barack Obama delivered one-liners while knowing that earlier he had approved the raid on Osama bin Laden's compound. His appearance that night became famous in that he was able to maintain a lighthearted manner while knowing the critical event that would soon follow. And he didn't even have to wear a mask.

CHAPTER 7

Evolution of the Civic Carnival

HISTORIC WANDERINGS

Steam-Powered 1870s Introduce a New Era

Although Carnival had long been celebrated in various forms, it became official, at least in the Christian world, in 1582 when Pope Gregory XIII included the pre-Lenten celebration in what would become known as the Gregorian calendar. The same document established the 365-day year that most of the world follows.

From the last half of the nineteenth century and through the first half of the twentieth century, national railway lines promoted Mardi Gras throughout the country. (From the collection of Peggy Scott Laborde)

Through the centuries, the celebration would be shaped by geography and circumstance and carried across the oceans in the age of exploration, but one decade, starting 288 years after Gregory's calendar was introduced, would take the celebration in new directions and perhaps secure its future. The history of Carnival is long and winding, but something major happened in the 1870s. In several places in the United States and Europe, existing Carnival celebrations were given a new look. The festivities were formalized. New traditions were begun.

Steam, when tamed and channeled, had given the world a new form of power, and that created novel and faster travel opportunities. Trains were taking people quickly, at least by the standards of the time, to places that they had never been to before. (In the U.S., the first transcontinental railroad was completed in 1869.) Although the term "economic development" was not used in the 1870s, that thinking was there. The decade can be described as giving birth to what might be called "The Civic Mardi Gras."

Carnival, in the boom time of the Victorian era, had a new purpose. No longer was its meaning, whether pagan or Christian, just spiritual. Enterprise was a new god. For better or worse, the Civic Mardi Gras gave Carnival a fiscal reason to exist and survive. Following are some examples from around the world.

The revival of papier-mâché artistry in the New Orleans Carnival has its roots in Viareggio, Italy, known for its own large-scale parades. Their Carnival celebration is organized by the Fondazione Carnevale Di Viareggio. Its symbol is a clown-like figure named Burlamacco, created by artist Uberto Bonetti in 1931. Burlamacco is dressed in a classic Commedia dell'Arte costume. This image is from a signed poster by Bonetti. (Courtesy of Jonathan Bertuccelli)

Arrival of Rex. There had been organized Carnival activity in New Orleans before 1872. The Krewe of Comus began staging its Mardi Gras night romp in 1857. The Twelfth Night Revelers started parading in 1870. For as long as Frenchmen walked the streets of frontier New Orleans, there had been often impromptu street celebrations as well as elaborate balls. However, in 1872, a new character arose. His name was Rex, and he would be the unquestioned King of Carnival. He would give Carnival its first lasting organized day parade on Mardi Gras Day and, in doing so, made more of an event out of Mardi Gras. Circulars tacked in stations up and down the railroad lines urged travelers to come to New Orleans to see the spectacle of the king of the Carnival. Rex gave the celebration its colors—purple, gold, and green—and its anthem, "If Ever I Cease to Love." Reconstruction still ruled in 1872, but Rex helped loosen the tension.

King Felix. Also in 1872, Mobile, Alabama, which had an established parading tradition that predated New Orleans', saw the ascension of its own

King of Carnival, this one known as Felix. Like Rex, Felix became a symbol for the season and gave a reason to visit the Mardi Gras celebrations. Felix, like Rex, would become a more politically neutral, people's-king character, though he never achieved the stature in his town that Rex has in New Orleans. Both cities in 1872 felt the need for a King of Carnival.

Mystic Society of the Memphi. Memphis too developed its Carnival in 1872, in the form of Memphi, a group founded by a former Confederate general. Taking notice of the economic success New Orleans was having with its Mardi Gras, the group also had the hope of salving Reconstruction's economic wounds. Suddenly there were new groups in three Southern towns trying to recover from a brutal war but also wanting to welcome the new age of travel opportunities.

Viareggio, Italy. Not all of the sudden surge in Carnival activities could be explained by Reconstruction recovery. In 1873, Viareggio took advantage of expanded railroad service along Italy's northwest coast to build a Carnival parading tradition. Shunning a king in a land where a real king, Victor Emmanuel II, sat on a throne, the founders chose a clown-like character named Burlamacco to become a symbol of the Carnival that is highlighted by an extensive parade along the town's wide beachfront promenade. (Americans, on the other hand, having rejected European-style royalty in their revolution, liked to emulate it in their celebrations.)

In 1960, the Rex organization sent New Orleans float-builder Blaine Kern to Viareggio to study that town's float-building techniques. Kern maintained contact with that town and, in 1977, hired Raul Bertuccelli, a member of a Viareggio float-building family, to work in New Orleans. Bertuccelli's son, Jonathan, would one day design Rex's Butterfly King float, which was introduced on Mardi Gras 2012.

Did Rex's arrival in 1872 influence the creation of the Viareggio Mardi Gras a year later? There is no evidence one way or the other, though ship travel between Italy and the port of New Orleans was frequent. Clearly, Viareggio influenced the float design of the New Orleans Carnival. The two towns on different continents may have ultimately nurtured each other.

Nice. Formerly part of Italy, Nice, the French Riviera's largest city, formalized its Mardi Gras celebration in 1873. Although the first mention of a Carnival-like celebration in the area dates back to 1294, the modern Carnival started the same year as Viareggio's and was highlighted by local artists putting grotesque figures on floats. Like Viareggio, Nice built elaborate floats from which flowers were thrown. There was no doubt deep-rooted historical grounding for maintaining Carnival, but it also boosted tourism during the down days of winter.

Philadelphia. What happened in the 1870s would create a model that would be used through the decades. Although Mummery, a European tradition of masquerading on New Year's Day, can be traced in America as far back as 1642 in Philadelphia, largely because of the Swedish influence in the region, in 1870 an attempt was made to organize the marching groups. (Michael Krafft, the founder in 1831 of Mobile's first continuing parade, the Cowbellians, was a native of the Philadelphia area and would have been used to New Year's Day parading, as was done with the first march of the Cowbellians.) In 1901, the city of Philadelphia took another step and created a city-sponsored event.

Venice. On Italy's Adriatic coast, venerable Venice had a Carnival tradition that can be traced back to 1162. As in many European cities that once celebrated Carnival, the festivities declined. In Venice, Mardi Gras was on the wane during the eighteenth century, and Benito Mussolini banned it outright in the 1930s.

In 1979, the Italian government and the local artistic community, hoping to capitalize on the town's history and culture, decided to rebuild the Mardi Gras there and established what was officially known as "Carnival of Venice." Just as earlier Carnivals had reorganized as railroads expanded, Venice's Carnival could take advantage of the passenger-jet age.

Through the centuries, Carnival would adapt to circumstances. In 1964, the passage of the Civil Rights Act in the United States opened the way for national chain hotels that had previously shunned the South to expand. In New Orleans, big names such as Sheraton and Hilton appeared in the skyline. They would help fund a convention and tourism bureau, which would in turn be a catalyst for expansion of the city's convention center. The Rivergate was built with freight doors high and wide enough to accommodate a new supersized parade named Bacchus. The new age of tourism opened by the arrival of the national chain hotels would help give birth to the superkrewe. Tourism-funded buildings, including the convention center and the Superdome, would give the krewes a place to hold their spectacles, and that in turn increased tourism.

With the advent of the Civic Carnival, some might say the season lost some of its innocence, but it also lost its vulnerability. No longer could anyone say that the season was irrelevant and a drain on communities. The numbers, both in dollars and euros, were too compelling. The parade was just beginning.

STORIES TOLD

A Visit to Viareggio

Not much good can be said about Benito Mussolini, except that he made the trains in Italy run on time. On this Sunday afternoon, we were counting on the former Italian dictator's legacy as we began a journey that would take us from the Tuscan hill town of Montecatini Terme to the seaside town of Viareggio. It was to Viareggio, home of the famous Carnevale Di Viareggio, to which, in the 1960s, the captain of the Rex organization sent a young float-builder named Blaine Kern to study float design. The big papier-mâché heads with moving hands seen in New Orleans parades, such as on Rex's jester float, reflect the Viareggio influence.

The family of Jonathan Bertuccelli, who sculpted Rex's Butterfly King float that debuted in 2012, is from Viareggio, Italy. (Photo by Dr. Stephen Hales)

Viareggio was not what I had imagined it to be. I had envisioned a quaint Italian village, sort of like the place where Geppetto made Pinocchio; instead it's a busy seaside resort. By the time we got there it was late afternoon, and the station platforms were filled with beachgoers, mostly kids, heading home. We, on the other hand, headed toward the beach. The walk was about ten blocks through the old part of town, which architecturally looks a lot like the French Quarter, with a similar mix of cafés and gift shops. I wasn't prepared for the waterfront, which I had envisioned to be a small Italian beach with grainy sand and a few ice-cream vendors along the road. Instead, it was more like Miami's South Beach. Hundreds of people strolled along the main boulevard, while others were in lounge chairs on the sand as the sun began its descent into the sea. There was the expected bustle of restaurants and shops, plus one peculiar statue—that of a clown wearing checkered pants, his arms outspread as though grasping for the world. He is Burlamacco, the symbol of the Viareggio Carnival. From his beachfront perch, Burlamacco can see the parades as they roll along the boulevard.

We took an early-evening train back to Montecatini, where we had a walk of about a mile or so from the train station to the hotel, much of it along the Avenue Giuseppe Verdi. The composer occasionally visited the town to experience its thermal baths. He too had an influence on our Mardi Gras, especially at the Carnival balls, where many kings and queens have made their entrances and exits to the stirring grand march from his opera *Aida*. Now we were making our own grand march. There was no orchestration, but at the café where we stopped for pizza, the sound of Chianti being poured in a glass was all the music we needed.

CHAPTER 8

Year of the Ordinance

HISTORIC WANDERINGS

Black, White, and Blue Ribbon

Sooner or later, the issue would have to be faced in a public forum. In 1991, sooner arrived, though many people were still hoping for later. New Orleans City Councilmember-at–Large Dorothy Mae Taylor introduced an ordinance that in effect called for the integration of Carnival krewes. The word "racism" hovered over the debate that followed, though it often obfuscated and added pain to a complex social issue that had less to do with race and more to do with tradition and government's role in regulating freedom of association.

Faced with a potentially explosive matter that quickly gained national attention, the City Council formed a blue-ribbon committee with the hope it could resolve the problem. (In government parlance, a blue-ribbon committee is an unpaid group set up to advise government on a specific issue. The committee has no law-making power. In the spirit of full disclosure, I will state here that I was appointed to that committee by Mayor Sidney Barthelemy, so my perspective is from the inside where, despite the perception of racial divisiveness as seen from the outside, black and white members worked hard to resolve an ordinance that some considered worthy but whose many parts few totally agreed with.)

It is important to understand that, at the time, the city had a black mayor, and the City Council had a black majority. As is true for most elected officials caught in a controversy, there was a public-posturing side and a behind-the-scenes side. City Hall wanted to calm tensions and preserve the lucrative Carnival season yet show some progress on what was seen as a civil rights ordinance.

Some parts of the proposed law were immediately removed with unanimous consent. Criminal penalties were stricken away; so too were prohibitions against discrimination by gender, so as to appease the women's organizations that were content with the way things were. (Attorney Sam LeBlanc recalled that, at one meeting, a member of the now-defunct all-female Krewe of Venus held a sign protesting the ordinance that read, "No Penis in Venus.")

Other changes included modifying

Municipal Auditorium, New Orleans, La.

From 1930 until Hurricane Katrina, the Morris F. X. Jeff Municipal Auditorium was the location of many New Orleans Carnival balls. Plans are under way for its restoration. (From the collection of Peggy Scott Laborde)

The Krewe of Proteus, which began parading in 1882, is Carnival's second-oldest parading krewe. (Photo © Mitchel Osborne)

the minimum group size, so as not to affect the all-black Mardi Gras Indians. The city's Municipal Auditorium (later known as the Morris F. X. Jeff Municipal Auditorium), where many private Carnival balls were held, was also exempted from the reach of the legislation.

In the end, the ordinance focused on krewes parading on the streets of New Orleans. Although it did not mention them by name, the law centered on the "old-line" organizations: Comus, founded in 1857; Rex, 1872; Momus, New Year's Eve 1872; and Proteus, 1882. Each had a reputation of being exclusive to white Anglo-Saxon males. Although most of the other krewes, with the exception of Zulu and the West Bank-based NOMTOC, were mostly white, they were of less concern to the ordinance's supporters.

Of the four old-line groups, Rex's situation was a bit different. Taking seriously Rex's role as the king of the Carnival, the parent School of Design organization has always seen his social responsibility differently. Rex's membership was believed to be more inclusive than that of his old-line brothers. As is true with all secret-membership organizations, outsiders are never sure who belongs and who doesn't, but Rex, by reputation, spread his arms wider. Indeed, during the controversy, the Rex captain even addressed the City Council, assuring that his organization was inclusive.

For the other old-line krewes, the issue may have had more to do with principle than racial attitudes. Unlike Rex, they operated with a blackball system similar to that long used by fraternal organizations and private clubs. Under such a system, prospective members do not apply but are recommended by members—any one of whom could cast a blackball and veto the recommendation. Blackballs can be issued for many reasons, most not having anything to do with race or religion. The system is inherently discriminatory but not necessarily racist. To Momus, Proteus, and Comus, the issue was one of big government telling them how to run their businesses.

Because the krewes paraded on public streets, their attorneys feared they would be vulnerable to the law. Secretive by nature, in the tradition of early men's clubs such as the Masons, the krewes were concerned that the ordinance would give citizens access to their membership information. Two of the krewes even stopped submitting their debutantes' pictures to be published in the daily newspaper, fearing that too would give the government leverage. Also lost was the longtime tradition of Rex toasting his queen in front of the Boston Club. Club leaders were concerned that being part of an event that utilized public space would raise similar arguments against them. The toasting was moved to the InterContinental New Orleans Hotel, on St. Charles Avenue, where it has been held since. (That change would in turn result in a shorter parade route.)

In a world governed by "tradition," the old-line groups felt they were being violated. One of Carnival's saddest moments came when Comus and Momus announced that they would not "leave their den" for the 1992 Carnival. A year later, Proteus did the same. Rex, ever the public servant, maintained his reign.

Rex officials worked behind the scenes to resolve the issue, as did the Boston Club, which hired prominent attorney LeBlanc, a former state legislator skilled in the ways of politics. He was associated with the firm Adams & Reese. Some of the best legal minds from other local firms also participated, as krewes had connections with the firms of Chaffe McCall and Jones Walker.

At a meeting in one of Jones Walker's high-rise conference rooms, the idea for what would become the new law germinated. Among those present were John Charbonnet, then the Rex captain; Beau Bassich, a longtime Proteus official who was also serving as co-chair of the mayor's Mardi Gras Coordinating Committee; Ron Nabonne, from the mayor's office; LeBlanc; other lawyers; and me. The message was that City Hall wanted to get the situation resolved but could not allow anything that would be perceived as a reversal of a civil rights ordinance. A pivotal moment came when one attorney, who—it is relevant to the story—was black, suggested what was originally described as a "check-off system." Under it, any krewe applying for its annual parade permit would have to put a checkmark by a statement declaring that there was nothing in its bylaws that mandated discrimination.

As the idea was discussed, it seemed to have legs. Nabonne, who was also black and who emerged as one of the pivotal behind-the-scenes players, said he would bring the idea to Mayor Barthelemy and key councilmembers. Eventually came the response: the mayor would approve it, as would the council, including Dorothy Mae Taylor, although she said she would "mau mau" before voting in favor. (In that context, "mau mau" refers to making, in the early civil rights style, a passionate speech condemning segregation.)

After much touching up of minor language details (the term "check-off" was eventually replaced with "affidavit"), the blue-ribbon committee (which had an almost equal number of black and white members) approved the plan. It was then brought before the council. Taylor made good on her promise to be vocal before casting her vote but then joined the majority.

The new law was thought to be an opportunity for the old-line krewes to return, but they thought differently. Their lawyers worried that because blackball systems

This Knights of Chaos float illustrated the frustration of many Orleanians after Hurricane Katrina. (Photo © Mitchel Osborne)

A Knights of Chaos float reflected post-Katrina angst. (Photo © Mitchel Osborne)

were inherently discriminatory, they could not sign an affidavit saying otherwise. The only way they could stay would be to change their procedures, but that would be a breach of tradition. They also worried about public reaction if they did return. Maybe one day, some of the members said, but the time was not right then.

Proteus did return in 2000, preceding Orpheus in its Lundi Gras night slot. In 2001, on the same evening known to Carnival aficionados as "Momus Thursday," a krewe that looked very much like the old Momus parade rolled out of the den that Momus shared with Comus and Proteus. This new krewe, which like Momus specialized in satire, and which used Momus's former floats, was called the Knights of Chaos. (Momus would continue staging a very private ball on that same Thursday night each year. Some Chaos members have been known to hurry to that ball after their ride.)

Comus never did return to the parade route, and that is Carnival's biggest loss. The sight of the old floats wobbling down St. Charles Avenue with the flambeaux casting a golden glow made a fitting end to Carnival. Comus, which started the city's continuing parading tradition, ended the parade season with its Mardi Gras night romp. This parade symbolically drew the curtain on Carnival. When Comus locked his den, Carnival lost its exclamation point.

Comus is still seen, though on television, during the annual Mardi Gras night broadcast of the Rex and Comus balls on WYES TV, Channel 12. The broadcast ends with a literal curtain closing, directed by the Comus captain.

In retrospect, it is clear that the ordinance had a major impact on Carnival. New krewes, anxious to show their inclusiveness, would form, particularly the superkrewe of Orpheus, which paraded in Proteus's former Lundi Gras night spot. In 2000, Muses would bring expanded opportunities to women. The satire void created by Momus's departure was first filled in 1998 by a sassy startup group cleverly named Le Krewe d'Etat. The krewe's first "coup" was securing the coveted Friday-night-before-Mardi Gras slot, parading along St. Charles Avenue behind the venerable Hermes parade.

Proteus's return and Momus's reincarnation took some of the sting out of the losses. Significantly, both were welcomed in their return by Marc Morial, a black mayor whose father, Dutch Morial, had always felt beholden to the Carnival krewes for supporting him, to the point that they canceled their parades during the divisive 1979 Mardi Gras police strike so that the strikers lost their leverage. (There too Rex had played a role, coordinating the support of the other captains.)

Though the ordinance caused much grief, it also raised some fascinating social questions. LeBlanc recalled the female groups that wanted to remain as such and the Mardi Gras Indians who did not want the law to violate their traditions. From an attorney's perspective, he said, the controversy "was fun."

Perhaps the biggest impact of the ordinance debate is that it brought forth an issue that would have to be faced eventually.

Because riders wear masks and because of the variations in skin-color shades in New Orleans, no one knows how racially mixed the krewes are, though certainly the superkrewes of Bacchus, Endymion, and Orpheus have always had minority members. Zulu has long had many white riders, most of whom are not part of the Zulu organization but are part of various float groups.

Ultimately, one law governs Carnival participation more than any other—economics. It comes down to the question of who can afford to ride in a parade and purchase items to toss from floats. Many krewes eagerly welcome any would-be rider willing to pay.

Overall, Carnival may be the most blissfully integrated urban celebration

A scene from the Young Men's Illinois Club Ball. Debutantes from the black community are presented at this ball. (Photo © Mitchel Osborne)

in the world, with each group having its own niche. The Mardi Gras Indians remain black, as they should be, though female participation is increasing (see more on these groups in chapter 12). Several gay Carnival organizations stage the season's most theatrical Carnival balls. Muses was not the first all-female organization but the first formed in the era when women were such a dominant part of the professional workforce. The krewe brought a whole new set of players into the season.

Then there is Carnival's indigenous music, primarily the early rhythm and blues classics frozen in time, including "Go to the Mardi Gras," "Mardi Gras Mambo," "Carnival Time," and "Big Chief." Black performers popularized them all. And for the past several years, Zulu visits Rex after the latter arrives at Riverwalk Marketplace on Lundi Gras.

The truth is that Carnival in New Orleans always had more soul than anyone realized.

When Zulu Helped Save Mardi Gras

During the bad days shortly after Hurricane Katrina, Mayor Ray Nagin went to Atlanta, where he met with a group of black displaced New Orleanians. Their lives had been uprooted, and the city's future was uncertain. Nagin tried to answer their concerns as best as he could. But what the night would be best remembered for was that toward the end of the meeting, one woman raised her hand and scolded that, with so many people displaced, nobody should be thinking about having Mardi Gras parades. Nagin, perhaps caught off guard, agreed.

His Honor might not have been thinking about the television cameras in the back of the room or the speed of modern communication or the significance of his nod in the affirmative, but the lead story on the ten-o'clock news in New Orleans that Sunday night was that the mayor was saying that there should be no Carnival celebration.

Coming at a time when the world's media were still camped in the city, the statement was beamed out internationally and presented as another example of a city so down on its knees that it could not stage a parade. New Orleans without Mardi Gras—perhaps the city was really dead.

After the mayor returned to New Orleans, he soon changed his position. Saying he was "outvoted" by the tourist commission on his Atlanta decision, Nagin declared that he now favored a modified parade schedule. (My research of the city charter has failed to discover any clause under which the tourist commission can outvote the mayor, but I think I understood his point.)

Now the question was how to modify the schedule. Most parades would have fewer floats, and their routes would be shortened. For many krewes, smaller was good, because they barely had the strength to put anything together. One group that was quite opposed, however, especially about the route shortening, was Zulu. Its officers spoke passionately about being allowed to parade in those neighborhoods with cultural links to the group. Zulu roared. It wanted to be on the streets at full strength.

There was dissention within the Zulu organization. One past king threatened to sue, saying it was inappropriate for the group to march. But the Zulu bosses were undeterred.

In the end, Zulu got its way.

The queen of Zulu traditionally wears an elaborate costume in the Mardi Gras morning parade. (Photo © Mitchel Osborne)

The king of Zulu wears a large feathered headdress during the parade. (Photo © Mitchel Osborne)

Budweiser Clydesdale horses are a fixture in many New Orleans parades, including Zulu.
(Photo © Mitchel Osborne)

Three years later, in 2009, Zulu celebrated its centennial. Within that century, Zulu has had few grander, or more important, moments than that first Carnival after Katrina. Imagine if Zulu had not paraded along its entire route. With so much media attention, and with the very faint heartbeat of the city being overly analyzed, the word would have spread around the globe: New Orleans now rolls parades through its white neighborhoods, while forsaking its black neighborhoods.

The truth is that lots of white folks were facing challenges then too, including many who feebly climbed on floats, some that were decorated with blue tarpaulins to spoof the recovery.

By taking a stand, Zulu helped save Carnival in 2006 and perhaps forevermore. Once the parades started, the message was spread that there was still life and joy throughout this battered city that had risen from its knees if only to yell, "Throw me something!" Anyone who paid attention might have learned that Carnival is not about racial divides but multiple cultures celebrating in their own way. With Zulu on the march, the Mardi Gras Indians could prowl their neighborhoods with a little more spirit; the bars in Treme could put beer on ice.

And those people in Atlanta, I suspect they celebrated too. Mardi Gras provides a good excuse to come home, if only for a day. When water rises, coconuts still float.

Zulu pages get ready for their big ride. (Photo © Mitchel Osborne)

This Zulu parade rider displays one of the krewe's more unusual throws. (Photo © Mitchel Osborne)

Zulu warriors in the Zulu parade. (Photo © Mitchel Osborne)

A Zulu krewe member gets ready to bestow his next coconut, a highly prized "throw" from the parade. (Photo © Mitchel Osborne)

America's WETLAND Presents
The Lundi Gras Blue Tarp Celebration

For the 2006 Mardi Gras season, many creative costumes were made out of blue tarpaulin material, the familiar covering for roofs damaged by Hurricane Katrina. The America's Wetland Foundation even staged a blue-tarp fashion show. (Photo © Mitchel Osborne)

Center: *Zulu coconuts are handed out to lucky parade-goers each year.* (From the collection of Peggy Scott Laborde)

PUMPING STATION

CANAL ST.

Many krewes presented a Katrina-themed parade in 2006. (Photo by Peggy Scott Laborde)

STORIES TOLD

Duke-Edwards: A Political Back Story to the Ordinance

In 1991, the state had been the center of global attention when former Ku Klux Klan Grand Wizard David Duke, at the time a Louisiana state representative, made it into a gubernatorial runoff against former governor Edwin Edwards. For many Louisianans the choice was tormenting. Edwards had a reputation for being effective but dishonest; Duke was an outspoken Klan leader. Duke's electoral popularity was not due entirely to his racial views, which he soft-pedaled. He spoke more about issues of economic equity that concerned conservative voters. Still, the thought of a former Klan leader being elected governor would have been devastating for the state's reputation. A slogan seen throughout the state pleaded, "Vote for the Crook—It's Important." Voters took that advice and Edwards was elected with 61 percent of the vote, a landslide defeat for Duke. Some saw that as an encouraging sign that the state stood strongly united against Duke. Others wondered why Duke made the runoff in the first place.

At the very least, the runoff vote salved a wound that the Carnival ordinance, introduced a few months later, would irritate. Here again, though, there was unity. Early polls showed that most New Orleanians, both black and white, were against the ordinance, at least in its original form. That may have accounted for the many adjustments made to the proposed law. Clearly, what voters of all skin colors wanted most of all was to get racial debates behind them.

For all the tension of the time, Edwards at least gave the era one of its all-time best quips. The former governor, who was legendary for his romances, commented that he and Duke had one thing in common: "We're both wizards beneath the sheets."

CHAPTER 9

Getting the Facts Straight

HISTORIC WANDERINGS

New Research Gives Different Insights

There's one problem with the history of the New Orleans Carnival as we know it. Much of it is wrong. Mythology, legends, and falsehoods get entwined with the truth at all levels of history, but for something as whimsical as Carnival—a season that gives emphasis to wearing a mask—the truth is especially disguised. New research reveals that the roots and reasons of Carnival are different, though no less fascinating, than originally explained.

Purple, Green, and Gold: The Real Story

Wherever Mardi Gras is celebrated throughout Louisiana, and the nation, its colors are purple, green, and gold. We know this about the colors—they originated in New Orleans with the first parade of the Rex organization in 1872. During the week before that inaugural parade, the local newspapers carried

Purple, gold, and green were first used in the Carnival celebration by Rex. A Rex or Comus flag indicates past royalty in that residence's family. (Photo by Peggy Scott Laborde)

proclamations issued by the newly created "King of the Carnival" declaring that balconies should be draped in those colors. Less clear is why Rex chose that combination. Through the years there have been many explanations, but never one that could be verified. The most common contemporary explanation has been that the colors stand for justice, faith, and power, but one might wonder why those qualities were so special to the Rex founders. Why not faith, hope, and charity? Or trustworthy, loyal, and helpful?

Not only is there uncertainty about the significance of those three words, neither is there certainty about their association with those colors. According to eighteenth-century antiquary Francis Grose's *Military Antiquities Respecting a History of the English Army, from the Conquest to the Present Time,* purple represented fortitude; green, good hope; and yellow, honor. Are these qualities any less desirable than justice, faith, and power? A book on *Signs and Symbols of Christian Art* has purple, green, and gold representing triumph, power, and pure light respectively. The meanings are clearly in the eye of the beholder.

A 1950 newspaper column by journalist/historian Pie Dufour in the *New Orleans States* seems to have popularized the "justice, power, and faith" explanation, although Dufour wisely did not totally embrace it. In an earlier column, he had stated that there was no acceptable explanation for the origin of the colors. A few days later, a local librarian drew his attention to Rex's 1892 parade, which had the theme "Symbolism of Colors." Each float displayed a color and a meaning. Floats seven, twelve, and eight depicted purple, green, and gold respectively, with justice, faith, and power, in that order, assigned as the meaning of each. A flowery statement issued by Rex, and published in the *Times-Picayune* that year, proclaimed those three words to be the meaning of the official colors.

Dufour wondered how the 1892 Rex members knew what was on the minds of the founders twenty years earlier. He suggested that the true reason for the color choice might be simply that they looked good and had, as a *Picayune* editorial on the eve of the first parade noted, a "delightful contrast." In the Rex centennial book, *If Ever I Cease to Love: One Hundred Years of Rex 1872-1971,* authors Pie Dufour and Leonard Huber further dashed the prevailing theory, although it would nevertheless survive. After telling about justice, faith, and power being linked to the 1892 parade, they argued: "This of course is an *ex post facto* explanation, and one may be certain that the colors were selected in 1872 because they were gay and colorful and not because of any symbolism as explained by Rex two decades later."

One reason that the origin of the colors has been so difficult to discover is that the Rex founders never offered any explanation. They called for the colors purple, gold, and green to be displayed but did not say why. That supports Dufour's and Huber's contention that the colors had no meaning. Surely if they did stand for something, the poetic philosophers among Rex's founders would have said so. But why those particular three colors? For that there has been no answer—until one-fourth of the way into Rex's second century while I was doing research for the Rex-sponsored book, *Marched the Day God: A History of the Rex Organization.* By asking enough questions and discovering enough answers, the explanation was found.

Finding the truth began with another question: why three colors? Why not one, or two, five, or ten? Was there anything significant to the number three? The key to that answer may have been hidden in the edicts issued by the Rex founders in the days preceding the first Rex parade and published in *The Republican.*

Those edicts contained good-natured verbiage that suggested Rex was a true sovereign. "His Royal Highness" issued orders preparing for his arrival. In the minds of the founders, a king must have a kingdom, and a kingdom must have a flag. All of the national flags that the Rex organizers would have been most familiar with—the United States, Great Britain, France— were tricolors. It was probably inconceivable to them that a flag should be anything else but a tricolor.

That resolved then, which three colors? Here we might assume that a certain three colors were immediately dismissed; red, white, and blue. Not only were those colors already taken by the above-mentioned nations (as well as the Confederacy), they were, ever since the Netherlands carried flags of red, white, and blue in its war against Spain, the colors of revolution and a republican form of government. Those colors were hardly appropriate for an absolute monarch such as Rex presented himself to be.

Given that there would be three colors, and that the founders probably ruled out red, white, and blue, what then should the colors be? One color seemed obvious—purple—for that color has traditionally been linked to royalty. From here, the selection process takes on a life of its own. The key word here, and one that has been missing from attempts to solve the colors' origin, is "heraldry." Dating as far back as the fifteenth century, the rules of heraldry governed the symbolism of coats of arms and hence flags and banners. The men of Rex, educated and steeped in the romanticism of monarchy, would have been familiar with and respectful of heraldry, which also governs color selections.

According to heraldry, the "fields" in a heraldic device should consist of "metals" and "colors." The metals are either silver, represented by white, or gold. And indeed every national tricolor has either white or gold. So for Rex, the question was should the metal be gold or white? The choice of gold seemed obvious, especially with white already in such common use.

Now with the metal settled, how about the colors? According to heraldry, there are only five acceptable choices: red, blue, purple, green, and black. With purple being a logical choice and with gold as the metal, Rex's final choice came down to two combinations: purple, gold, and green or purple, gold, and black. The choice seemed obvious.

But now there's a concern. According to heraldry, a metal should never touch another metal and a color should never touch another color. It would be improper, for example, for a flag to be red, blue, and white. Yet, Rex's field is often spoken of as being purple, green, and gold, a heraldic *faux pas* placing a color on top of a color. Does this disprove the heraldry theory? No, it supports it, because . . . in the days preceding the first Rex parade, when the royal edicts were published, the field, as first mentioned in Edict XII, was stated as being, in this order, "green, gold, and purple." Over time, the order of the colors would be changed in popular verbal usage, yet when Rex first pronounced them, they were in perfect heraldic sequence. (The combination of colors does have the extra benefit, as Dufour and Huber suggest, of looking good together.)

Could there be another answer to the meaning of the colors? Perhaps, but any other answer would have to contend with the colors fitting so perfectly into the rules of heraldry.

What, then, should the simple answer be when the colors' origin is questioned? The problem is that the answer is not simple, certainly not as simple as "justice, faith, and power." But the truth only strengthens Rex's monarchical status. As for all great sovereigns, his colors are based on the laws of heraldry.

Case closed.

This City Had a Major Influence on Our Carnival

Philadelphia, cradle of American democracy, is surfacing as the most important city in the development of the American Carnival. Not only that, but while there are European connections to this nation's Mardi Gras celebrations, they may have been, in the early days, more from Sweden of all places, than France.

Philadelphia in antebellum America had a major influence on the South. It was one of the richest and closest cities to the South. From there, people, ideas, and traditions flowed easily.

Known of course as the city where serious debate led to the Declaration of Independence, Philadelphia had a frivolous side as well. The Liberty Bell may have rung in July 1776, but on New Year's Day, miscellaneous bells and other noisemakers were heard along the city's streets as a group called the Mummers paraded. A 1981 article in *Smithsonian Magazine* explained it as follows:

> Historically, the New Year's Day Parade results from a blend of cultures that thrived in the city from the early half of the 17th century through the early part of this one. English roots go back to 15th century Christmas Mumming Plays. (Mumming comes from the German word *Mumme*, meaning disguise or mask.) Local tradition has it that as early as the 1620s the Swedes and Finns in Tinicum—now a southwestern section of the city—celebrated the New Year by shooting off guns (they were often called "the shooters"), banging pots and pans, and making a clamor as they visited neighbors after Christmas.

Another article published by a Mummers string band also traced the European origins of mummery: "It started in the late 1700's. When the Swedes came to Tinicum, just outside of Philadelphia, they brought their custom of visiting friends on 'Second Day Christmas,' December 26." According to the article, the Mummers later advanced their period of celebration to include New Year's Day and rang in the new year with masquerades and parades of noisy revelers. Especially revealing was the article's reference to Momus, a mythological character who was also part of the New Orleans Mardi Gras: "The traditions of other nationalities were also present. The use of masks and different costumes were carried over from the Greek celebrations of King Momus, the Italian-feast of saturnalia, and the British Mummery Play."

Just as America would be a melting pot of people, the city that was the country's cradle would become a melting pot of celebrations. In Philadelphia, the post-Christmas festivities took the form of the Mummers wearing costumes, making noise, and parading on New Year's Day.

Now the scene switches to Mobile, Alabama, the town that we are told is responsible for New Orleans' Mardi Gras parading tradition. It was there that on New Year's Eve night 1831 a group of men, including a one-eyed reveler named Michael Krafft, was about to step into history.

Perry Young, in his classic book, *The Mistick Krewe: Chronicles of Comus and His Kin,* told of a dinner that night at a downtown Mobile restaurant organized by Krafft. The celebrating continued well past midnight: "At the approach of dawn they continued their frolic on the streets and at the important hardware store of Griggs, Barney & Company encountered irresistible temptation in the shape of rakes, gongs, cowbells, and horns which early-morning clerks had displayed in front of the store. The young gentlemen armed themselves with these rakes, cowbells, horns, and perhaps, some other instruments, and proceeded to parade on the streets with clang and clamor."

A group of maskers on St. Charles Avenue in 1905. (Photo by Alexander Allison, courtesy of the Louisiana Division/City Archives, New Orleans Public Library)

It may be that the events were less spontaneous than they appeared to be. Young might not have known, or appreciated the significance of the fact, that Krafft was from Philadelphia. Krafft would have been very familiar with a tradition of parading and hell-raising on New Year's Day. In his own way, he brought mummery to Mobile, where it would metamorphose into a group called the Cowbellians. Gradually, their march would be institutionalized and shifted to coincide with the French celebration of Mardi Gras. The history of celebrations is that of one culture building on another. That's what was happening as the American Carnival evolved.

Next we go to New Orleans, where the celebration of Mardi Gras had been mostly lavish balls and sorry street spectacles. As Young reported, some Mobile Cowbellians came to this city and didn't like what they saw. Drawing on their Cowbellian knowhow, they were part of the group that, in 1857, established the Mistick Krewe of Comus. That was the beginning of the New Orleans Carnival parading tradition as we would know it—a tradition that would become part of the universal image of Mardi Gras.

As Young so poetically put it:

The seeds sown by Michael Krafft have persisted. His mystic progeny are legion. Many have appeared on the scene and disappeared after periods of varying success.

But they are copies, not of a carnival which once held sway in Italy or France, but of a pageantry initiated by Krafft and his gay fellows, and deftly fitted into the ancient Carnival of New Orleans by an evolution of its own.

In New Orleans, the Philadelphia influence would be felt in many ways. Fifteen years after the first Comus parade, Mardi Gras would be crystallized as a major celebration in New Orleans by the founding of the Rex organization, in 1872. Two of the founders, E. C. Hancock and C. T. Howard, were from Philadelphia. As we have seen, Rex was founded primarily as a cure for Reconstruction and to coordinate into one the miscellaneous groups that had been parading on Mardi Gras. In Philadelphia, the sentiment was shockingly similar, as noted in the string band's article: "In the 1870's the nation was recuperating from a Civil War and what had been an uncoordinated group of neighborhood celebrations turned into an area wide parade with two main groups of participants." Might Hancock and Howard been inspired to found Rex by the news from back home?

Philadelphia's Carnival influence may have also spread out into the Atlantic. In the Bahamas, a celebration called the Junkanoo takes place each New Year's Day. For the occasion, locals dress in costumes and join marching clubs to parade and celebrate. Written histories suggest African links, and there may be, but the Mummer influence is overwhelming. In colonial days, the Bahamas were governed by the territory of the Carolinas. Ships from Philadelphia would have made many stops on the islands. Junkanoo is probably mummery with an African spin. Curiously, Junkanoo and Comus may have had common ancestors.

Rex Was Not Founded Just to Entertain a Grand Duke

Legend has it that the parade of the King of Carnival was created in 1872 as a last-minute effort to entertain the Russian Grand Duke Alexis, whose visit to the city would coincide with Mardi Gras that year. Legend misses the point. None of the early accounts of Rex's formation mentions the Grand Duke as the reason for the first parade.

One person who should have known the truth was Lewis Salomon, the cotton merchant who was the first Rex. In 1921, he was interviewed by a *Times-Picayune* reporter on Rex's upcoming fiftieth anniversary. Speaking of the founding, Salomon said something that was quite revealing: "Carnival was being talked about, when the war was over, as a sort of tonic for the wearied South."

That sentiment was being shared elsewhere. In the same year that Rex was founded in New Orleans, the Mobile Carnival Association was formed, and the Mummers were reorganized in Philadelphia. Embattled cities were using Mardi Gras to unite their populations and draw more tourists. They were doing it with or without the presence of a Grand Duke.

As for Alexis, New Orleans would have had a King of Carnival without him, but the Carnival was nevertheless blessed by his attendance. His being here added romance to Rex's triumphal entry and legitimized the Carnival king's claim to the throne, as one royal acknowledged another. It also gave the Grand Duke Alexis a place in history, though probably not where he expected it to be. He would forever be far better remembered in New Orleans than in St. Petersburg or Moscow.

Opposite: Recent historical research by the author indicates that Mummers from Philadelphia influenced the Mobile Mardi Gras, which in turn influenced the New Orleans celebration. The Krewe of Orpheus has invited the Joseph A. Ferko Mummers String Band to play in its parade. (Photo © Mitchel Osborne)

French Catholic by Tradition but Yankee Protestant in Implementation

While the French, bless them, brought the phrase "Mardi Gras" to the New World, and French settlers informally celebrated the day, the parades were largely a Protestant creation. Among the last names of the founders of Comus were Todd, Addison, Shaw, Ellison, Churchill, Lay, Smith, Hanning, Wood, Conyers, Ellis, Ross, Ferguson, Newton, Campell, Murphy, and Butler. There is not one recognizable French name in the bunch.

Among the Rex founders, the key person, E. C. Hancock, a descendent of John Hancock, was not likely Catholic. Lewis Salomon, the first Rex, was Jewish. The others had mostly Anglo-Saxon names. One early Rex, George Soule, was a descendent of the pilgrims who arrived on the *Mayflower*. Soule was from New York; Hancock and fellow founder C. T. Howard were from Philadelphia. Not even the first Rex was a native—Salomon was from Mobile.

Curiously, this phenomenon of Protestants embellishing a Catholic holiday is not unique to New Orleans nor this country. I once spoke to a Dutch sociologist who had studied European Carnivals. He noted that there were several Catholic villages where the Protestants had been the main force behind the Carnivals. Why? One possible explanation is that the Protestant work ethic introduced an entrepreneurial spirit into Carnival by creating an event to boost local economies. Remember too that Anglo-Saxon cultures had a tradition of post-Christmas winter celebrations. As the world expanded, their festivity would be absorbed under the French term "Mardi Gras." And finally, though the French Catholics have the image of having a good time, Protestants want to have fun too.

Lundi Gras Is *Not* an Old Tradition

Explanations of Lundi Gras too frequently say that the tradition traces back to 1874, when Rex began arriving in New Orleans by the Mississippi River. Those arrivals stopped in 1917. So Lundi Gras is usually described as a revival of an old tradition

In fact, though it quickly became widely used, the phrase "Lundi Gras" was not commonly part of the local Carnival language until 1987. (Zulu would eventually establish a major Lundi Gras presence by creating its own arrival ceremony and staging a riverfront festival, but it did *not* start the Lundi Gras tradition.) In '87, Rex did revive his river arrival, but that was only part of the new Lundi Gras festivities, which included fireworks, concerts on the river, and, for several years, Proteus marching down Poydras Street toward the river.

Prior to 1987, the night before Mardi Gras was just known as the night before Mardi Gras. From 1874 to 1917, Rex's arrival was never referred to as Lundi Gras. The accurate

A young reveler with her first pair of beads on Mardi Gras Day.
(Photo © Mitchel Osborne)

The king of Zulu visits with Rex during the annual Lundi Gras festivities at Riverwalk Marketplace. In 2013, William H. Hines was Rex and Cedric Givens reigned as Zulu. (Photo by Peggy Scott Laborde)

The captain of Rex, Rex, and Zulu meet annually during the Lundi Gras celebration. (Photo by Peggy Scott Laborde)

statement would be to say that Lundi Gras started in 1987 as a series of events that included the Rex arrival. Accurate statements, however, sometimes have a hard time getting recognized.

STORIES TOLD

Heraldry and War

During the Battle of Manassas, Gen. P. G. T. Beauregard of New Orleans became concerned that the Confederate troops did not have an appropriate battle flag, so he sent word for one to be designed. Several designs were submitted, including one from E. C. Hancock, a New Orleans journalist who years later would be one of the key figures in the founding of the Rex organization. Aiding Beauregard in the selection was a former staff member, Col. William Porcher Miles.

The colonel rejected one of the favored designs because it was contrary to the laws of heraldry. He suggested instead a flag that was similar to Hancock's proposal—red, with blue bars and white stars. From this incident, we learn two things about future Rex founder E. C. Hancock. He had an interest in designing flags, and he was aware of the laws of heraldry.

THE COLORS GO TO LSU

Not only did Rex influence the colors of the nation's Carnival celebrations, but he would influence LSU. There are variations in the story of how the university adopted purple and gold as its colors, but the common thread is that the colors came from Carnival. A generally accepted version of the story is that in 1893 some LSU football players, in anticipation of the team's inaugural season, were looking for ribbons to adorn their gray jerseys. A Baton Rouge store had stocked Carnival colors for the upcoming season—or at least two-thirds of the colors. The green had not arrived yet.

So, the players settled on purple and gold. (Since the team's first game was to be against Tulane, green may not have been a popular choice anyway.) Curiously, one of the players, quarterback Ruffin Pleasant, would have even more decisions with statewide implications ahead of him. From 1916 to 1920, he would serve as governor of Louisiana.

CHAPTER 10

Birth of the Superkrewes

HISTORIC WANDERINGS

Bacchus Premieres

It was spring 1968, and something was brewing over dinner at Brennan's restaurant other than café brûlot. Restaurateur Owen "Pip" Brennan, Jr., the son of the restaurant's founder, had a hankering to start a new Carnival parade and, on this evening, was meeting with some of the big boys in the Carnival establishment. What sort of impression would he make?

"I had never met Blaine Kern in my life," Brennan recalls about the area's most prolific float-builder. "I told [costume designer] Larry Youngblood that I would like to meet Kern and tell him about the idea we had been talking about. So Larry arranged this meeting, and he, Blaine, and I had dinner at the restaurant one night. I said, 'Blaine, we would like to put the finest parade on the streets that we can possibly do. We would like to have very large figures; we're going to have the best bands we can get. We want to have the best lighting we can get, and we want to have a celebrity king.' And we talked through dinner, and he got excited. But then he went home and told his wife, 'You know, I met Owen Brennan's son tonight, and he's crazy. You ought to hear what these guys are talking about doing; they don't have a chance.'"

Less than a year later, in February 1969, the premiere Bacchus parade took to the streets. It featured a celebrity king and the biggest floats ever seen in the New Orleans Carnival, built by Kern.

By the standards of Carnival history, Bacchus is still a neophyte, outdistanced by nearly a century by Rex and Proteus and decades behind such parading stalwarts as Babylon, Hermes, Thoth, Iris, Carrollton, and Mid-City. But Bacchus has made up for its youth by its size and the dramatic impact it has had on the celebration. Through the years, the krewe has created an event so enormous in scope that the once-forlorn Sunday night before Mardi Gras has become, to those who speak the parlance of Carnival, "Bacchus Sunday."

By now the basics of the Bacchus story are well known. A group of businessmen who were concerned that the New Orleans Carnival had become stale and was declining as a tourist attraction wanted something new, big, and different to attract visitors to the city. They broke tradition by inviting a celebrity, rather than a krewe member, to be a king. They called for bigger floats built around themes that were more popular and less literary than those of the old-line krewes. They did away with the social element, even to the point of not having a queen or court. And they followed their parade not with a formal society ball but a bash held in a convention hall so big that the oversize floats could be paraded into it. (Originally the event was presented in the former Rivergate, which is now the

The Krewe of Bacchus, founded in 1968, originally held their post-parade galas at the Rivergate, New Orleans' first convention center. (Photo © Mitchel Osborne)

site of Harrah's Casino. It is currently held in the Ernest N. Morial Convention Center.)

Bacchus caused such a sensation that many new krewes, particularly in the suburbs, would try to imitate it, though only two, Endymion and Orpheus, would succeed. Bacchus was the first of the "superkrewes." (This writer coined the phrase in the *Gambit* weekly newspaper under the *nom de plume* of the original Rex Duke parade critic. It was necessary to create this new category under which parades of Bacchus's size could be critiqued.) Carnival would forever be different because of what Bacchus brought.

Historic Links

Bacchus developed legions of fans. But it also had its detractors, who complained that Bacchus represented the "Americanization" of Carnival and that its towering floats with fiberglass figures were out of scale and out of step with the artistry of the old-style floats. August "Augie" Perez, one of the group's founders, once offered a more ecumenical perspective. "We felt there was a need for this kind of parade," he said. "We actually support the old historic things, and I personally am very hurt that some of the old things that we had don't exist anymore. Some of those old parades and those old clubs meant a lot to us and are part of our history. I think New Orleans has got to hold on to its history—hold on to it tight."

In fact, Bacchus has more historic links than perhaps its leaders, critics, and boosters realize. For one, Bacchus is one of three influential krewes founded on Royal Street or its extension. In 1856, after an initial meeting at an Uptown pharmacy, the organizational meeting for what would be the Mistick Krewe of Comus was held at the former Gem Café and Oyster Bar, in the 100 block of Royal, only three blocks away from present-day Brennan's. Beginning in 1871, the formative meetings for the Rex organization were held in the St. Charles Hotel, located at the site of the Place St. Charles building in the 200 block of St. Charles, which is the street Royal becomes once it crosses Canal Street. The birthplace of the three krewes spans six blocks down the same thoroughfare.

Secondly, there is more of a kinship in spirit between the early founders of Rex and those who started Bacchus than has ever been realized. Rex, which first paraded in 1872, was founded partially as an effort by local businessmen to attract visitors back to a city that was suffering through postwar Reconstruction; Bacchus was started by businessmen to bring visitors back to a Carnival that was suffering from lethargy. There were also rooms to fill, because the passage of the Civil Rights Act in 1965 had opened the way for the national hotel chains to move in. Rex expanded Carnival by creating an opportunity for participation by those who had not necessarily been a part of the high-society parades that existed at the time, Comus and the Twelfth Night Revelers. Bacchus expanded the opportunities for participation, as well, just as other krewes, such as Babylon and Hermes, had made camaraderie, rather than social standing, a prerequisite for a ride. The history of Carnival organizations is that of gradual democratization as new groups expand participation. Had Pip Brennan, Augie Perez, and the other Bacchus founders been alive in 1872, they would have fit in among the founders of Rex.

Curiously, the first Rex parade and Bacchus had something else in common—celebrity royalty. The Russian Grand Duke Alexis's presence at the first Rex parade likely drew a larger crowd for the event. Bacchus turned out the crowd for its first parade by having a celebrity, entertainer Danny Kaye, as its monarch. Like Rex, Bacchus would become an attraction unto itself, but Alexis and Kaye are linked by being the first Carnival celebrities of their eras.

Bacchus, for all its innovation, is, like all Carnival krewes, an offspring of Comus (although in mythology it was the other way around: Comus was an offspring of Bacchus). The wine god's floats may be bigger and star studded, but the style of parade is similar to that first one minted by Comus on Mardi Gras night 1857. All else to follow would be influenced by that parade.

Two Captains

Just as in Comus, the Bacchus krewe captain would serve as the pivotal person in the organization. Brennan held that job from the beginning. But then disaster struck hard. In 1980, one of Brennan's daughters, Leslie, and her son, whose first name was Brennan, were killed in a car accident outside Atlanta caused by a drunk driver. "It really took a lot out of me," Brennan says. "So I went to Augie, and I went to the board and asked if he could take over." Perez, a prominent architect whose résumé includes phases one and two of the convention center, Canal Place, the InterContinental New Orleans Hotel, the LL&E Building, and the 1984 World's Fair, served as captain from '82 to '89, when Brennan returned to the job. He says, however, that Brennan was never too far from the decision-making process.

While Pete Fountain has spent many a Mardi Gras leading his Half-Fast Walking Club, he has also appeared with some of the superkrewes. Here he is a celebrity grand marshal in an Endymion parade. (Photo © Mitchel Osborne)

Pete Fountain's Half-Fast Walking Club began in 1961. (Photo by Peggy Scott Laborde)

Saints quarterback Drew Brees, having just led the team to a Super Bowl victory, reigned as Bacchus in 2010. (Photo © Mitchel Osborne)

Actor Will Ferrell wore the Bacchus crown in 2012. (Photo © Judi Bottoni)

Bacchus's Bacchagator pays tribute to an inhabitant of Louisiana swamps. (Photo © Mitchel Osborne)

As is true with all parades, there were challenges. "One time, when Jim Nabors was king, we were chased by the rain and tremendous wind; I mean, it was really blowing," Brennan recalls. One year, though, a different thunder was heard. In 1979, all parades in Orleans Parish were canceled because of a strike by members of the New Orleans Police Department. A few New Orleans krewes, including Endymion, paraded in Jefferson Parish that year, but some, including Bacchus as well as Rex, Proteus, Momus, and Comus, chose not to parade at all rather than leave the city. Bacchus that year, Ron Howard, ruled over a party rather than a parade. The theme "The Undersea World of Bac-chu-steau" was carried over to the next year, when Pete Fountain reigned.

Celebrity monarchs, like political ones, have ruled to mixed reviews. Both Brennan and Perez agree that former "Moses" Charlton Heston was one of the most gracious to ever reign. But then there were the ones who were more moody and cranky, such as Billy Crystal, William Shatner, and a very fatigued Jackie Gleason. Brennan laments that there are more obstacles now to landing celebrities than in the early days. "Sometimes the insurance companies stick their nose in it. They get a little concerned about their piece of property coming to Mardi Gras and getting up on that float."

Of all those who sat on the throne, it is the first one, Kaye, who will always hold an extra-special place in Bacchus history. "We had known him well as

Baby Kong (shown here), King Kong, and Mama Kong are among the popular signature floats of the Krewe of Bacchus. (Photo © Mitchel Osborne)

a customer and a friend," Brennan recalls. "When we contacted him, he, of course, didn't know what we were talking about. So, when we told him what we were trying to accomplish, he said, 'Sure, I'd love to do it.' He flew his own private plane here, flew it himself. We met him at the airport. It was freezing that first night, and he said, 'Man, I'm gonna freeze up there. What am I gonna do?' So we rigged up an electric blanket, plugged it in the float. But when he saw the crowd, he never even thought about that blanket. He never even sat down!"

Through the years, Bacchus has developed its own celebrities in the form of its menagerie of annual signature floats, which now includes the whale-like Bacchawhoppa, Baby Kong, the Bacchasaurus, and the Bacchagator. The latter made its mark in local Carnival history by being the first tandem, a float consisting of two or more units attached to each other. Perez, ever the architect, had a hand in creating the gator after getting inspired in an unlikely setting. "I was in an airplane. I was looking down and watching the little baggage cars come around. You know there are six to eight baggage cars behind a tractor. I noticed how the cars followed each other (each turning at the same spot where the previous one turned). So I investigated how they did that and took the exact same system and incorporated it on the float." There was already an alligator head waiting for a body. The head had made its initial appearance in New Orleans at the 1984 World's Fair, having been built by Kern to decorate one of the entrances.

As the gator crawls into the future, where will the krewe take it? "We're not looking to get any bigger," Brennan said in 1998, on the occasion of the thirtieth anniversary of the krewe's founding. "We're not looking to add any more floats, although we might be doing another signature float somewhere down the road."

In 2012, there was a bump in the road. Some members, angry over a significant dues increase, discovered records showing high salaries and travel allotments given to krewe management, which included members of Brennan's family. The revelations flew in the face of Carnival tradition, where captains and key non-staff organizers serve without pay. Several tense meetings were held.

While no one could deny Brennan's importance in reshaping Carnival, the controversy did raise questions about the economics of parades, particularly those of the superkrewes. By the time Carnival season arrived, the issue, reportedly, was resolved. Brennan remained at the head of the group, and the parade was ready to roll.

Bacchus has overcome bumps before, but with grandeur comes attention. Like the floats, even their controversies are bigger than most. Also bigger than most are the crowds that Bacchus continues to draw. That crazy idea discussed over dinner at Brennan's revitalized Carnival.

Enter Endymion (Again)

Anniversary dates for the Krewe of Endymion are like Mexican independence days—there are options from which to choose. Just as the Mexicans can celebrate

The Krewe of Endymion holds concerts near the staging area for its parade. In recent years, it has dubbed the event "Samedi Gras" (Fat Saturday). (Photo © Mitchel Osborne)

independence from Spain and independence from France (plus revolutions against an occasional dictator), Endymion had two births. The first was in 1966 when the group was founded (or should it be '67 when it first paraded?), and the second was in 1974 when it was born again. That was the year the organization blasted to the top of the Carnival scene after changing from a routine, little-noticed, Gentilly-based parade to a megakrewe that is now the largest in all of Carnival.

By the early seventies, when Endymion was between lives, Carnival was experiencing its own revolution, inspired by Bacchus's success. Bacchus's influence was so enormous that practically every fledgling krewe at the time promised to be "like Bacchus." None succeeded except Endymion (and then eventually Orpheus), which not only became like Bacchus but also went on to establish a character of its own.

Endymion is the only krewe to have more than one thousand members. (Not counting organizations that are really a confederation of many groups, such as the truck parades in New Orleans and the samba pageants in Rio de Janeiro, Endymion is, quite probably, the biggest Carnival parade club in the world.) Bacchus does not have a queen; Endymion does, and the Endymion king is not a celebrity but a krewe member. The krewe's fans do see stars, though: they are scattered throughout the parade as grand marshals and miscellaneous riders. The celebs then perform at Endymion's party that evening.

Endymion introduced the succession of mini-floats carrying feather-bedecked maids and dukes—an innovation that other krewes have tried to imitate, often as a substitute for real floats, with far less success. For Endymion, the mini-floats

Endymion's queens wear elaborate headdresses during the parade. (Photo © Mitchel Osborne)

are just a prelude to the larger segment of the parade to follow. Endymion has become a master of prelude—so much prelude that one year the elapsed time, with only occasional brief stops, between the arrival of the lead police unit and the king's float was one hour. This is a multi-beer-run parade.

In most New Orleans Carnival organizations, the captain's identity is traditionally kept secret. There is no such custom in this group. Few parades are as identified with one person as Endymion is linked to its captain and founder, Ed Muniz. A former radio-station owner by trade, he is the only person to have ruled in two different parishes with three different titles: two civil, one royal. He was a Jefferson Parish councilman and mayor of Kenner and is a New Orleans parade captain. For one night a year, he lords over the city, most often while having a stand-in wearing the plumage-laden captain's outfit, with its top-heavy feathery crown. That allows the real captain to ride in a lead unit, less bedecked but more capable of being in control of the action.

Muniz is part of a genre of guys who were raised with New Orleans' culture and tradition, later moved to the suburbs, but tried to elevate the city's offerings. Near where the Endymion parade turns on to Canal Street is the Centanni home, once decorated annually with Christmas lights and displays. Little Al Copeland was among the city's kids who would each year gawk at the spectacle. He resolved to put on such a display himself one day, and in the suburbs, he did. Muniz remembered the Carnival parades of his youth and wanted to bring something bigger and better to the city.

What he has brought is more a street festival than a mere parade. As someone

Borrowing its title from the Jerome Kern tune, Endymion's "Ol' Man River" float was among the earliest to use fiber-optic lighting. Note the trumpet-blowing water nymph. (Photo © Mitchel Osborne)

who lives near the Endymion Canal Street route, I can attest that "Endymion Saturday" is like no other day of the year. The entire neighborhood is gridlocked by traffic and barricaded streets as early as two o'clock, leaving those of us who are entrapped with little else to do but party. For a few hours of one day a year, old city streets are like what they used to be before air conditioners and television, when people walked those streets and mingled easily. Some reclusive neighbors are only seen on Endymion Saturday.

At its best, the parade is like a really intricate movie, with so many scenes and subplots that it needs to be watched several times to absorb. In 1998, Endymion introduced, without the fanfare that it deserved, a new permanent float to its collection. Built as a tandem so that it can turn corners, the float is entitled "Welcome to the New Orleans Mardi Gras." It was a marvelous addition that is visually busy and carries 150 riders. The new float was the largest in all of Carnival at the time. Some entire krewes do not have as many members as the number who ride on that one float.

Whatever records that float held were shattered in 2013, when Endymion introduced "Pontchartrain Beach, Then and Now," an eight-part tandem float so big that the tractor that pulls it is capable of tugging a 747 aircraft. LED lighting bars were designed to create a feeling of action. The unit is more than 330 feet long and capable of carrying 230 riders. The frame and solid rubber tires can support forty tons (including eleven tons of throws). Not only did the float introduce dazzling lighting but also the capacity to create smells typical to the former lakefront amusement park. For all the spectacle, there was also a classic bit of captain's prerogative. One unit depicts sunbathers along the beach's shore, commemorating where Muniz met his wife-to-be.

Endymion is named after a shepherd boy who was a mythological symbol of youth. Through the years, the krewe has maintained its youthful ambition. It does so because there was once a boy in Gentilly whose dream was Olympian in size. That's all the more reason to lift a goblet, perhaps filled by the wine god Bacchus.

Orpheus Ascending

In 1993, what would be the trinity of superkrewes was rounded out with the debut of Orpheus, which parades on the night before Mardi Gras in the spot previously held by Proteus, which dropped out temporarily after the Dorothy Mae Taylor ordinance controversy. Entertainer Harry Connick, Jr. was announced as the founder, with the day-to-day work handled by theater director Sonny Borey. Orpheus's first signature float was the "Smokey Mary," a train-like tandem built in recognition of the rail service that once ran between the French Quarter and Lake Pontchartrain. In 1998, Orpheus introduced the Leviathan, a dragon-style three-unit tandem that was the first New Orleans Carnival float to fully utilize fiber optics. The new krewe also mastered old-style lighting by

The Krewe of Orpheus's "Smokey Mary" float honors a legendary train from the nineteenth century that ran up Elysian Fields Avenue. (Photo © Mitchel Osborne)

During one of its parades, the Krewe of Orpheus paid tribute to Comus, the oldest organized Carnival krewe. Comus's symbol is a cup. (Photo © Mitchel Osborne)

This Krewe of Orpheus float illustrates the krewe's efforts to incorporate nineteenth-century designs. (Photo © Mitchel Osborne)

The Krewe of Endymion holds its annual Extravaganza in the Mercedes-Benz Superdome.
(Photo © Mitchel Osborne)

creating its own flambeaux torches. Of the superkrewes, Orpheus is the only one open to men and women as riders. Just as Bacchus has its after-the-parade spectacular at the convention center, so does Orpheus with its Orpheuscapade.

In 2000, Proteus resumed its Monday march, preceding Orpheus along the route. Instead of being hurt by sharing its night with Orpheus, the older krewe has been helped, because two krewes attract more of a crowd than one. The vintage Proteus parade, with its classic nineteenth-century look, combined with Orpheus, which has established itself as the prettiest of the superkrewes, makes Lundi Gras night a visual feast. Those in the crowd who look past the beads and at the floats can see the best of more than 150 years of float design.

Celebrity riders have always been a part of the superkrewes, though with mixed success. Bacchus featured a celebrity monarch from the beginning, delivering big names in its first few years including Raymond Burr, Perry Como, and Bob Hope. Endymion's king is selected from among its membership by lottery. The big names usually ride Endymion's floats as grand marshals or just special guests, most often to perform at the post-parade extravaganza. Orpheus at first shunned royalty but in some years has featured multiple "celebrity monarchs." (In 2013, Harry Connick Jr., rode as a co-monarch with jazz musician Troy "Trombone Shorty" Andrews and actor Gary Sinise.) Of all the celebrity pursuits, Bacchus's is the most demanding, because having a single throne-riding king around whom a publicity machine is built takes more of a commitment. A grand marshal could miss a parade, and few would notice; an absent king would be conspicuous.

But the truth is that celebrity monarchs might not be needed. As the superkrewes have marched through the ages, they have become the stars.

STORIES TOLD

Endymion's Uptown Visit

There are two combinations in life that defy the natural order. One is a basketball team called the Jazz playing in Salt Lake City, and the other is Endymion parading Uptown. The former situation continues to exist, contradicting both geography and logic. The other has happened occasionally, the first time being in 2002, when construction to return the streetcar to Canal Street forced the mammoth Endymion from its natural path to the well-worn trail along St. Charles Avenue. It has happened again due to weather, such as in 2011, when a nightmare scenario forced Endymion to roll on Sunday night after Bacchus.

Endymion Uptown is as out of place as it was in 1979, when a police strike in the city caused the krewe to flee to the suburbs, where non-union sheriff's deputies guarded the parade route. Like a rogue elephant suddenly beamed to the Arizona desert, the lumbering giant did not belong.

The degree to which there has been an excess of Mardi Gras can be measured by the relative droopiness of the oak trees along St. Charles Avenue. As the area becomes oversaturated by Carnival, the trees' branches are dragged down by the grosses of beads that were intercepted on the way to their intended targets. By the Saturday night before Mardi Gras 2002, with the messenger god Hermes having triggered a long weekend of parades the evening before, the oaks, laden with strings of beads, looked as though they manufactured spaghetti rather than acorns. That should have been an ominous sign to the natives, who were already oblivious to the lost eleventh commandment declaring, "Thou shalt not have the march of the pagan god Endymion along the same trail already claimed by the pagan gods Bacchus and Orpheus." The commandment did not even take into consideration Zulu, Rex, and the bead-happy truck parades that bring Carnival to a close on the following Tuesday.

In other years, native dwellers near Canal Street, used to Endymion's impact on their environment, knew that by two o'clock on parade day, they would be blocked in by traffic and would not be free until near midnight. But Endymion was the only giant in their forest, so its presence had been endured, even enjoyed. Uptown, where by this weekend the drains are already cluttered with escaped doubloons and the budding azalea bushes are pocked by plastic cups, needs a reprieve from more floats.

Mid-City, usually aglow on the Saturday before Mardi Gras, was sober that night in 2002. The Orleans Avenue neutral ground, where tribes of bead-gatherers would camp out the evening before in order to snag a good spot for the parade, was as quiet as a burial ground. Each year that Endymion rolls on Orleans Avenue, the thoroughfare reverts to being a joyous camping ground, as though nature and the spirits are once again aligned.

By parade time 2002, Endymion began to meet its Waterloo along Napoleon Avenue. The first hour or so of the march moved smoothly, but the floats in the back had trouble crossing the ramp at the Napoleon Avenue Wharf loading area.

There were breakdowns and delays, none of which would have mattered to the weary crowd had there not already been two parades in the neighborhood earlier that day. Only the police and sanitation workers on the late shift knew the exact bewitching moment when the last Endymion float turned off the route. Sunday, though, was near and, with it, more parades.

Endymion has more riders than any other krewe, and they are generous with the throws, but anthropologists say that Homo sapiens' necks can only endure so many pairs of oversize beads at once. Were it not for the protection of the bead-snatching trees, the species might be truly endangered.

Several krewes once marched along the Canal Street route; now all have moved Uptown except Endymion. Those krewes would be appreciated in a neighborhood where the trees have been bead-free for too long.

CHAPTER 11

Music to March By

HISTORIC WANDERINGS

When Rex Met *Aida*

Cairo, Egypt, and New Orleans share the same latitude, 30 degrees, which makes both towns sort of steamy and subtropical—places where vegetation and the spirit sprout, even in the winter. That was certainly the case in 1871, when an event in Egypt would forever become part of something that was germinating in New Orleans.

To celebrate the opening of the Suez Canal, the ruling khedive had commissioned an opera to be staged at the Cairo Opera House. Chosen as the composer was one of Europe's biggest names, the Italian Giuseppe Verdi. After some delays, the premiere performance was staged Christmas Eve of that year.

Appropriately, Verdi's opera had an Egyptian theme set around the tragic story of a captured Ethiopian princess (Aida) who falls in love with an Egyptian military commander and the conflict that causes with the pharaoh.

Verdi composed a lavish opera filled with what would become some of the genre's most cherished music, none more so than the stunning piece that was performed in act 2, scene 2. Beginning with the blare of trumpets, a cast of seemingly hundreds, many dressed as soldiers, royalty, and plain Egyptian folks, moved in procession across the stage to the stirring sounds of what was to be known as the "Triumphal March" or, more commonly, the "Grand March from *Aida.*" Never had music captured the spirit of victory more than Verdi's masterpiece march. If opera were war, Egypt could have ruled the world.

That same month in New Orleans, a group of young men was having meetings at the St. Charles Hotel. Like Verdi they too were on a mission to create something new, only in this case it was a parade that would debut only a few weeks later on February 13, Mardi Gras 1872. The new parade would be different from Comus and Twelfth Night Revelers. It would be held during the day, and the ruler would be the people's monarch, the King of Carnival. More simply, borrowing from the Latin word for "king," he would be Rex.

His Majesty's first parade was in itself a triumphal march. The procession became an annual event that would eventually include its own ball on the evening of Mardi Gras, where a debutante, to be known as the Queen of Carnival, would promenade with Rex around the floor.

Back in Europe, *Aida* was a major hit, being performed in the continent's grandest theaters. The opera reached the United States in November 1872, when it was staged at the Academy of Music in Manhattan. Although New Orleans was a major opera center, the Verdi composition, according to local opera historian Jack Belsom, was not performed here until December 6, 1879, at

In addition to serving as a home to opera, the French Opera House was the scene of many early Carnival balls, including Comus's. It was built in 1859 and burned in 1919. (From the collection of Peggy Scott Laborde)

The foyer of the French Opera House. (Courtesy of The Historic New Orleans Collection)

the French Opera House, by the touring Strakosch Italian Opera Company. "Thus it was sung in the original Italian rather than in French," Belsom says. "It was sung a total of three times that season but was not enthusiastically received because of less-than-adequate singers and decors. Things changed drastically the following season, when the excellent De Beauplan French Opera Company was in residence. They gave *Aida* a spectacular production, the sets based on designs from the original premiere, and with a strong cast. The first staging was on December 16, 1880, and it was done often that season, to acclaim."

That season created the setting for a most unusual opera incident. Mardi Gras 1881 was on March 1 and, according to Belsom's research, Rex had special plans for the night before. "The papers reported that on the previous evening (February 28), during a performance of *Aida*, Rex made an appearance at the French Opera House in mid-performance 'before the third act was over, being escorted to the royal box by De Beauplan, a guard of honor and lackeys with torches, to rounds of applause, and the royal anthem "If Ever I Cease to Love," which the orchestra struck up.'" Thus when Rex and *Aida* met, Rex's anthem, for the first and only time, was injected into Verdi's Nile scene.

In the world of Carnival, Rex is a powerful monarch, and that incident showed just how powerful. He was able to interrupt an opera with the obvious support of the event's organizers. One might suspect, as is true today, that the men of Rex were on many important boards, and in this case demonstrated some stroke in the theater as well.

For whatever the connections might have been, *Aida*'s presence seemed to have touched off a wave of Egyptian mania around town. A year later, in 1882, when the Krewe of Proteus made its debut, the ball's theme was "Egyptian Mythology."

One more curiosity: depending on who is doing the counting, the debuts of *Aida* and Rex are even closer than originally believed. Verdi did not consider the Cairo performance to be the official premiere. He protested that the event was a closed affair and not open to the public. To Verdi, the real premiere was when his opera opened at the glistening La Scala opera house in Milan. Not only were there general-ticket sales, but also, unlike in the Cairo presentation, superstar Teresa Stolz, an operatic hot number whom Verdi had in mind when he wrote the lead role, performed. The date of that event was February 8, 1872, five days before the Rex debut.

Historic parallels are little more than a collection of trivia unless we learn from them. The sagas of *Aida* and Rex give a glimpse of the sense of style among the better-educated men of the Victorian age. Schooled in the classics and raised with a sense of mission, they also faced numerous battles. Aida, the character, suffered from slavery, lost love, discrimination, and war. The men of Rex, living during Reconstruction, had in the previous decade experienced the hardships of

The French Opera House had a horseshoe seating configuration. (Courtesy of The Historic New Orleans Collection)

This rare photo shows a 1903 ball held at the French Opera House commemorating the centennial of the Louisiana Purchase. (Photo by John N. Teunisson, donated by George Schmidt to The Historic New Orleans Collection in honor of Blanche Mouledoux Comiskey)

a great civil war. Now was the time for peace and civility. For the moment, two rivers, the Nile and the Mississippi, flowed as one.

There is one more date to note in this saga, and that is Mardi Gras evening 1882. That's when the Rex organization and the Mistick Krewe of Comus first staged what would become familiarly known as "the Meeting of the Courts." We do not know for sure what music was played, but we do know that by that year the "Triumphal March" was a hot number perfect for such occasions. We know for sure that in modern times, Rex responds to two marches: his own, "If Ever I Cease to Love," and the march from *Aida* as he and Comus and their queens circle the floor in what is Carnival society's high holy moment.

By circumstance, Rex and *Aida* are contemporaries, having made their debuts only fifty-one days apart in different parts of the world but along the same latitude and each in recognition of ceremony and royalty. And their triumphs continue.

STORIES TOLD

Doc Souchon, Jazz, and Satchmo

His daughter was going to be Queen of Carnival, yet one of his idols was riding as king in the Zulu parade. What to do? Which one to see? That was the predicament local musician and physician Edmond "Doc" Souchon faced on Mardi Gras morning 1949. His daughter was named Dolly Ann Souchon. His idol was named Louis Armstrong.

Through some precise scheduling, Souchon was able to serve both monarchs. He missed the limousine ride with his daughter downtown so that he could see Armstrong arrive by boat on the New Basin Canal, and then he scurried back to his family in the Rex entourage.

Doc Souchon's morning was symbolic of a pivotal moment in the evolution of two of New Orleans' greatest cultural contributions, the American Carnival and jazz. For many years the two traveled separate paths, having nothing to do with each other. Ultimately, they could not be kept apart.

A story is told that in 1915, some officials of the Krewe of Comus were worried that younger people had lost interest in their tradition-laden society balls. To entertain the kids, the krewe, on Mardi Gras evening of that year, arranged for a special dance to be held at the Pickwick Club. Although the old-liners looked down on some of the newly emerging spontaneous music forms such as ragtime, a group of Tulane University students known as the Six and Seven-Eighths String Band was hired for the gig. The group played a lively type of music that was becoming the vogue. The kids enjoyed dancing to it so much

By the late twentieth century, the Rex organization, also known as the School of Design, began to once again issue elaborate invitations, as the krewe once did over a hundred years ago. This invitation for the 2000 "reception," as it is more formally referred to, was designed by artist Patricia Hardin. (From the collection of Peggy Scott Laborde)

The Marine Corps Band New Orleans performs at the Rex Ball each year. (Photo © Mitchel Osborne)

Rex and his queen begin the Grand March. The music selection is the "Triumphal March" from the Verdi opera Aida. (Photo © Mitchel Osborne)

Opposite: *Trumpeters announce the arrival of Rex and his queen at the Rex Ball.* (Photo © Mitchel Osborne)

that they opted that evening to stay at the dance rather than go to the ball. The band's sound was part of the evolution of a music that would eventually be known as jazz.

Although Carnival initially snubbed the music, jazz gradually conquered not only the world but its hometown Carnival, too. In 1966, Rex introduced a float called "His Majesty's Bandwagon," which featured a jazz band riding atop. By '68, three jazz groups were rolling with Rex. The old-line krewes, with their smaller-scale parades, were ideal for the brass bands and ragtag jazz groups that marched along with them. As Carnival expanded, so did jazz's prominence, with a defining moment being the 1949 reign of Armstrong, the music's greatest figure.

Even at the high-society Carnival balls, where jazz was once regarded as a bastardized art form, the dance selections began including the music. There was even a nativity inspired by the two forces. The birth date of the New Orleans Jazz Club was listed as Mardi Gras 1948.

One person would carry the cause through the decades. Among those students who played in the Six and Seven-Eighths String Band back in 1915 was Edmond Souchon, who, as an adult, would become known as "Doc." One of the best-known versions of Carnival's anthem, the nineteenth-century ditty "If Ever I Cease to Love," was recorded with the raspy-voiced Doc Souchon doing the vocals—set to jazz time.

A 1968 book published in honor of the city's 250th anniversary proclaimed correctly, "Only the city which produced jazz could have evolved New Orleans' Mardi Gras of today." Jazz and Carnival: Doc Souchon never ceased to love either one of them.

The Rex lieutenants and their wives lead off a Rex Ball tradition with the Grand Curtsy. (Photo © Mitchel Osborne)

Former first lady Laura Bush was a guest at the Rex Ball in 2010. (Photo by Estelle Egan deVerges)

The Captain of Comus and his lieutenants arrive at the Rex Ball with an invitation to Rex, his queen, and court to visit the Comus Ball. (Photo by Mitchel Osborne)

Opposite: *A maid in the Rex Court wears a blue sash and pin in a starburst design.* (Photo © Mitchel Osborne)

Even though members of the Mistick Krewe of Comus don't parade, they still dress in costume during their ball. (Photo © Mitchel Osborne)

Comus carries a cup instead of a scepter during his namesake ball. This mythological deity was known for offering sips from his cup to strangers, who would be transformed into half-man, half-beast creatures. (Photo © Mitchel Osborne)

Opposite: *Departing from the Rex Ball, currently held at the Sheraton New Orleans Hotel on Canal Street, the Rex captain leads Rex, his queen, and court across the street to the Marriott Hotel, the current location of the Comus Ball.* (Photo © Mitchel Osborne)

The Meeting of the Courts of Rex and Comus first occurred in 1882 and still takes place annually. (Photo © Mitchel Osborne)

Comus, Rex, and their queens share the throne at the Comus Ball after the Meeting of the Courts. (Photo by Estelle Egan deVerges)

Since the late 1800s, Carnival krewes such as Rex have bestowed gifts, or favors as they are known, to female family members and friends. (From the collection of Peggy Scott Laborde)

This favor is a Rex ducal. (From the collection of Peggy Scott Laborde)

A Comus krewe favor. (From the collection of Peggy Scott Laborde)

A Rex krewe favor from 1903. (From the collection of Peggy Scott Laborde)

A Rex krewe favor from 1907. (From the collection of Peggy Scott Laborde)

CHAPTER 12

Into the Future

HISTORIC WANDERINGS

Carnival's Rebirth

On February 19, 1980, Mardi Gras evening, something special happened in front of Gallier Hall, though few people were there to see it. Comus, rolling toward closing another season, stopped to be toasted by Mayor Ernest "Dutch" Morial. Joining Comus were platoons of New Orleans policemen, wearing their dress blues, who were marching or riding motorcycles in the parade. Comus, the mayor, and the police all toasted one another. As per custom, the champagne glasses were thrown down to the street, and the parade proceeded.

That was a decisive moment in the future of Mardi Gras in New Orleans. A year earlier, there had been no parades because of a contentious police strike. Morial had stood firm against the strike's organizers; the krewes stood behind Morial.

As the champagne glasses broke, so too should have many stereotypes. Morial was the city's first black mayor. Comus was often sneered at as being a symbol of the white elite. The police had been the renegades. But in this moment, they were all together, all celebrating.

When there were no parades in '79, many locals who had taken Carnival for granted realized what they were missing, and tourism operators felt the loss also. Carnival was very much the soul of the city.

Mardi Gras 1980 proved to be a rebirth. When that season ended, a new era of growth for Carnival began. There would be bumps along the way—the Dorothy Mae Taylor anti-discrimination ordinance in '92, rebuilding from Katrina in 2006—but Carnival remained strong. The whistles blew. The drums got louder. The march continued.

FUTURE WANDERINGS

Carnival's New Players

Carnival could be a metaphor for modern life in New Orleans: in the early 1990s (when the Taylor civil rights ordinance was an issue), the "levees broke" for Mardi Gras. Some krewes never returned, new krewes were started, and the parade calendar was dramatically changed. In some ways the changes were for the better, but in other ways there were painful losses.

Four krewes—Comus, Proteus, Momus, and the all-female Venus—stopped parading in the wake of the ordinance. (Venus's demise might have been due to other reasons. While the other groups survived as ball organizations, Venus stopped altogether.)

With spots to fill on the parade calendar, and with the City Council very eager to show its support of Carnival, existing krewes began to jockey for better timeslots—the Knights of Babylon parade shifted from their longtime slot of Wednesday to Thursday—and new groups applied. Of the latter, three would make their mark on Carnival in a big way: Orpheus, Le Krewe d'Etat, and Muses. Two others, Ancient Druids and Knights of Chaos, would help restore the traditions of Carnival.

Orpheus: • Year first paraded: 1993

• Founding captain: Sonny Borey • Parade slot: Lundi Gras night, behind Proteus • Classification: Superkrewe; male and female riders • Characteristics: One of the prettiest parades in all of Carnival; certainly the most attractive of the superkrewes. In the spirit of the old-line krewes, themes tend to be literary. The parade usually has a good mix of marching groups. Signature floats include the tandem "Smokey Mary" and the "Leviathan," which was one of the first to fully utilize fiber-optic lighting.

Le Krewe d'Etat: • Year first paraded: 1998

• Founding captain: Identity kept secret • Parade slot: Friday night before Mardi Gras, behind Hermes • Classification: Satirical traditional night parade; male riders • Characteristics: Has taken satire to a new dimension by having

Le Krewe d'Etat Dictator's Banana Wagon was inspired by a Carnival wagon once used by Bruno's Bar. (Photo © Mitchel Osborne)

sculpted figures on floats rather than traditional cartoonish cutouts. Some of the satire can be wicked. For a monarch, there is a dictator rather than a king. Signature floats include the Dictator's Banana Wagon, patterned after such a wagon once used during Carnival by Bruno's Bar. Among the marchers is the krewe's own internal group, the Dictator's Dancin' Dawlins. The krewe built its own flambeau torches.

Muses: • Year first paraded: 2001

• Founding captain: Staci Rosenberg • Parade slot: Thursday evening before Mardi Gras, behind Babylon and Chaos. • Classification: Traditional night parade; female riders. Leans toward satirical. • Characteristics: Famous for opening the way for many independent marching groups. Has very innovative krewe themes and throws, including hand-decorated women's shoes. The float depicting a high-heeled shoe is one of Carnival's most popular signature floats. The Muses glow ball coming down the street is an awesome sight. This krewe's parade is a real crowd favorite.

Ancient Druids: • Year first paraded: 1998

• Founding captain: Penny Larsen (instead of "captain," Druids uses the term "consultant") • Parade slot: Tuesday before Mardi Gras, before Nyx • Classification: Traditional night parade; male riders • Characteristics: Most unusual about this parade is that it was created by Carnival krewe organizers for the benefit of other parade organizers. Its maskers all wear druid costumes. Instead of a king, there is a high priest.

Knights of Chaos: • Year first paraded: 2001

• Founding captain: Identity kept secret • Parade slot: Thursday before Mardi Gras, behind Babylon. • Classification: Old-line-style satirical parade; male riders • Characteristics: Chaos represented the turmoil created by Momus's departure. Using Momus's floats, the krewe looks, feels, and even marches at the same time as the former satirical parade. It is a study in the historic preservation of the old-style Carnival.

A float from a Knights of Chaos parade laments the reduced printing schedule of New Orleans' longtime daily newspaper. (Photo © Mitchel Osborne)

Other krewes started during this period, including Pygmalion, Morpheus, and King Arthur, and the future will prove their worthiness. Besides the krewe shuffle, another significant change during this time was in the nature of the routes. Owing to the police department's wish (demand) for a uniform route, all East-Bank Orleans Parish krewes, except Endymion, now march along St. Charles Avenue, including three with names that are specific to another part of town: Carrollton, Mid-City, and Pontchartrain.

Gone also is the single-slot parade—again, except Endymion. The police have found it more efficient, for the use of barricades and personnel, to channel

The king of the Knights of Chaos, with his jester by his side. (Photo © Mitchel Osborne)

The Krewe of Mid-City stages the only parade that uses foil on its floats.
(Photo by Harriet Cross)

several parades in a row along a common route, so that all parades are part of a double-header or more. For the krewes, the changes have been mostly positive. St. Charles Avenue is Carnival's most popular route, and being part of a procession with other krewes helps attract bigger crowds. The Friday before Mardi Gras, when Hermes, Le Krewe d'Etat, and Morpheus all parade, has developed Bacchus-size crowds. The night of the Babylon-Chaos-Muses trifecta is also attracting large numbers. Making its debut in 2012, another all-female krewe, Nyx, would expand on the excitement created by Muses.

In 2000, Proteus returned to its Monday slot, now preceding Orpheus. With Chaos taking the place of the fallen Momus, Carnival was closer to being whole again. Still missing, though, was the Mardi Gras night romp of the Mistick Krewe of Comus. As is true with everything in New Orleans, recoveries are seldom total.

Black Street Culture Post-Katrina

There was plenty to worry about in the days after Hurricane Katrina's wrath, survival being first on the list. Not too many notches down, however, especially in New Orleans, was saving local culture. New Orleans is a town rich in character.

Much of what becomes culture starts in the streets, as it did when the musical improvisations of poor blacks and struggling Italians began to mingle and produced jazz. Outcasts often band together. Early blacks in New Orleans also found some kinship with area Choctaws, who were out of the mainstream as well. The cultures mingled. The most visual manifestation was the Mardi Gras Indians. For male blacks, this was a chance to be a part of a group and to direct talents in a creative way. Their feathery costumes were influenced by the style of the Plains Indians, whom they saw perform at traveling Wild West shows. From the local men's Afro-Caribbean heritage evolved a music form that was itself a Smithsonian-worthy bit of culture.

The two best-known tribes, the Wild Magnolias and Wild Tchoupitoulas, would make recordings. The latter, having connections to the Neville family and the group the Meters, recorded an album of their chants. The former, most identified with Big Chief Bo Dollis, recorded an early single of "Handa Wanda," as well as albums, and have toured extensively. The White Eagles and Creole Wild West also continue the Mardi Gras Indian tradition, the latter with a name that blends the tradition's multicultural origins and the Wild West shows that influenced the costumes.

By the time of Katrina, the number of Mardi Gras Indian tribes was on the wane, but when it is threatened, culture often proves to be resilient. Once the most private of Carnival-related groups, the Mardi Gras Indians transcended the back streets to become a global symbol of the recovery. The challenges of a Mardi Gras Indian chief were even a plotline in the HBO series "Treme."

There is evidence that the tradition is thriving. There are nearly forty tribes of various sizes. The tradition of the Indians making a post-Carnival appearance, on the Sunday nearest St. Joseph's Day (March 19), is now branded as "Super Sunday." Some tribes make a third appearance at the New Orleans Jazz & Heritage Festival, which can bring global recognition.

When Interstate 10 was built along North Claiborne Avenue, much of the vitality of the predominantly black neighborhood was lost. Another challenge to the culture occurred as people moved to other neighborhoods, leaving the old customs behind. Nothing endangers traditions within minority communities more than assimilation into the general population. Two groups that were once part of the black Mardi Gras almost perished but today are making a comeback. One is Skeletons, and the other is the Baby Dolls.

Men dressed as skeletons once prowled the Treme neighborhood on Mardi Gras morning, with the intention of frightening folks in a good-natured sort of way. (Skeleton costuming is common in many cultures, most famously in Mexico's Day of the Dead celebrations.) A 2003 nationally broadcast documentary, produced by filmmaker Royce Osborn through public-television station WYES, included haunting footage of some Skeletons.

The Skeleton tradition can now be seen outside of Treme as well. Le Krewe d'Etat, whose symbol is a skull wearing a jester's cap, is led each year by a group called "The Skeleton Krewe," whose costumes resemble the early bony ramblers. Another mixed-race group, the Bywater Boneboys, prowls the streets on Mardi Gras.

Where skeletons roam, so too do the Baby Dolls, a group of black women dressed as babies. Started in 1912, the practice suffered a falloff similar to the Skeletons, but in 2012 the group's centennial was celebrated. Organizer Millisia White's Baby Doll Ladies of the New Orleans Society of Dance, Inc., carried the torch to revive the tradition. Antoinette K-Doe, the flamboyant wife of the super-flamboyant R&B singer Ernie K-Doe (self-proclaimed "Emperor of the Universe"), is credited with originally resuscitating the tradition in 2004.

On Mardi Gras 2009, the Dolls' big day was dampened when they learned that Antoinette had died that morning. To her credit, a new generation of the emperor's universe has learned about the Baby Doll tradition.

Down in New Orleans, the recovery continues. Should you be in the right place at the right time on Mardi Gras morning, you might see the Mardi Gras Indians, Skeletons, or Baby Dolls. The yearning to preserve the culture has been a powerful force. In the end, Katrina did not conquer.

Flambeaux's New Age: The Yearn to Burn

Charles Andrews, the late captain of the Krewe of Sparta, came back from a flea market one day with a purchase that would be the envy of just about anyone in the Mardi Gras world. He had spotted twelve vintage flambeaux, the type traditionally used to illuminate New Orleans' Carnival parades. According to the current captain, speculation is that the flambeaux traced back to the builder of those used by Comus. "Some people think we stole them from Comus," the captain noted, only half-joking, "but no—they are ours."

So it happens that on the initial Saturday night of the parade season, Sparta is the first parade each year to introduce flambeau lights to the streets. As the parade forms along Napoleon Avenue, a krewe officer walks down a line of flambeaux. Each is held by a carrier recruited for the evening, who, with a torch, lights the two jets on each unit, thus performing one of Carnival's most picturesque ceremonies.

Flambeaux have illuminated many New Orleans parades since the nineteenth century.
(Photo © Mitchel Osborne)

Sparta is one of six krewes to own its own flambeaux, in its case a modest but impressive 12 kerosene-fueled torches, of which 6 to 8 are used in the parade. By far, the lord of flambeaux is the Krewe of Proteus, which has charge of 125 vintage flambeaux that were once shared with the Mistick Krewe of Comus. Two flambeau wagons can hold 48 devices each, making a total of 96 that are useable. Of those, Proteus and Chaos each use 30 in their parades.

All the above use flambeaux that, like the New Orleans Mardi Gras parading tradition itself, trace back to the nineteenth century. There is, however, a new wave of flambeaux in Carnival. Endymion, under the patented name of "Flambeaux New Orleans," has its own collection of modern propane-lit flambeaux that one krewe member described as being like a "barbecue grill on a pole." Ignition is almost as easy as flipping a switch. This superkrewe and Bacchus each use sixty flambeaux, while Muses asks for thirty. Orpheus too has its version of flambeaux, seventy-six of them, which are shared by Babylon, Hermes, and Morpheus.

When Le Krewe d'Etat was formed, much research went into creating their original forty-four one-of-a-kind torches. Key to a flambeau torch is the burners. The krewe's royal torch builders discovered ideal burners made in India that were used for cooking. They use mineral spirits as fuel and have a low flashpoint, which, according to a krewe official, reduces the risk of fire. Various local companies put together the tank, poles, and reflectors. Even the holster used to carry the torches required a special design by Arabi Slings and Riggings, a company that makes netting and cargo straps.

Once lit, the torches burn for about three and a half hours, just right if the parade runs on time but a problem if there is a breakdown along the way. Those who carry the torches get an undisclosed fee plus tips. (The hiring of flambeau carriers can get competitive. There have been stories about krewes parading on the same night trying to outbid each other for carriers. Once the flambeaux are lit, the police are vigilant about not allowing the carriers to move to another parade.)

In 2012, Le Krewe d'Etat started its parade with all forty-four of its flambeaux. At the end, though, there were only forty-two. Two carriers had walked off, carrying their poles. One krewe member explained that that had happened before; a carrier showed up at another parade with a Le Krewe flambeau. In 2012, the krewe member was optimistic about the possibility of their return: "We just hope that they show up again at our parade."

But maybe by then, they had run out of mineral spirits.

Gay Carnival: The Revival

No element of the Carnival celebration embraces the spirit of the Saturnalia as effectively; no variation has such a spirit of abandon; nowhere else are queens as adorned and adored.

Gays have been a part of the Carnival scene from the beginning, many times as part of the creative force behind the festivities. However, it was not until 1958 that the first openly gay Carnival ball, the Krewe of Yuga, was staged. In 1962, the event was raided and shut down by the police.

Gradually relationships, and legal representation, would improve so that, by the 1980s, there were as many as eight gay or lesbian balls on the calendar. Having faced social obstacles at the beginning, the gay Carnival scene has since faced obstacles of other sorts. AIDS took a serious toll, diminishing the number of participants and groups. Hurricane Katrina scattered some of the population and damaged the St. Bernard Civic Center, long the site of many of the balls.

The Krewe of Satyricon, a gay Carnival organization, is famous for its elaborate costumes. (Photo © Mitchel Osborne)

Nevertheless, the gay community's commitment to both the city and its Carnival remains strong. The openly gay Carnival is flourishing again.

Among the survivors are the Krewes of Amon-Ra, Armeinius, Mwindo, Petronius, Satyricon, and Queenateenas and the Mystic Krewe of the Lords of Leather, which boasts of being "the only leather-oriented Mardi Gras krewe in the world." The groups stage the most lavish, theatrical, and, some would say, outrageous balls in all of Carnival. After Katrina, these krewes had to scramble for ball sites because both the St. Bernard facility and New Orleans' Municipal Auditorium were closed. With the help of FEMA, the St. Bernard location has returned, now known as the Frederick J. Sigur Civic Center. Once again, the unlikeliest of jurisdictions, conservative St. Bernard Parish, is the epicenter of the gay ball scene.

While the balls are by invitation only, the street scene is wide open, especially on Mardi Gras at the corner of Bourbon and St. Ann streets. Crowds gather inside, outside, and on the balcony at the Bourbon Pub & Parade. A costume contest at that intersection, often dominated by costumes from the Krewe of Armeinius, accounts for many of the elaborate classically gay costumes seen on the streets.

There is nothing subtle about the gay Carnival, and that is to its credit. The straight path is seldom the most interesting.

Carl Mack, left, reigned as the queen of the Krewe of Satyricon. Trixie Minx, right, is a well-known New Orleans burlesque artist. (Photo by George Long)

A scene from the Krewe of Satyricon Ball. (Photo © Mitchel Osborne)

The Bourbon Street Awards gay costume contest, created by Clover Grill owner Arthur Jacobs, has taken place since 1963. (Photo © Mitchel Osborne)

Lundi Gras: The Making of a New-Old Tradition

There are some old traditions in Carnival. There are also some traditions that are thought to be old but really are not. One of the latter is the use of the term "Lundi Gras." While the practice of Rex arriving in New Orleans by boat on the day before Carnival is an old but interrupted custom, discontinued in 1917, the popular use of the term "Lundi Gras" dates back only to 1987.

In 1986, a musical called *Staggerlee* was staged at the Toulouse Theatre in the French Quarter. The show, written by New Orleanian Vernel Bagneris, was set in a black Creole bar in New Orleans on the night before Mardi Gras. Playing off of French patois, the dialogue had one of the characters refer to the evening as "Lundi Gras," the Monday equivalent of Fat Tuesday. Other than an early use of that term in a history of the city by Alcée Fortier, it was totally obscure.

Here the storytelling becomes awkward because, well, I started the Lundi Gras celebration while serving as a member of the city's Mardi Gras Coordinating Committee. I had seen *Staggerlee*, was struck by the phrase, and brought it to the table at a subcommittee meeting of the group. I felt that there needed to be a new downtown attraction on the evening before Mardi Gras. The Mississippi River, the source of the city's life, at the time had no role in the city's major cultural celebration. With the emergence of a downtown riverfront reconfigured for leisure rather than heavy commerce, there seemed to be new possibilities. A highly visual, early-evening event on the day before Mardi Gras could help draw attention to the riverfront and the urban Carnival. A secondary reason was to help Proteus.

Up until 1917, Rex would arrive on the Mississippi River at the foot of Canal Street and lead a small procession over to Gallier Hall, which was the city hall at the time. (Photo by John Tibule Mendes, courtesy of The Historic New Orleans Collection)

On the Monday before Mardi Gras 1986, during a steady rain, the krewe had paraded before a thin crowd. The emergence of superkrewe activities on the Saturday and Sunday nights before Mardi Gras was making locals weary by that Monday night. If Proteus would agree to alter its route to include a loop down Poydras Street to the river, that could reinvigorate that evening.

Riverwalk, a "festive shopping center" then operated by the Rouse Company, had recently opened along the riverfront. I knew of the company's interest in downtowns and local traditions. The idea then was to see if Rex would agree to again arrive by boat and if Riverwalk would agree to stage the event at Spanish Plaza, an adjacent public space within the shadow of the World Trade Center. Riverwalk would also provide entertainment and fireworks. The city would provide security as needed. During my pitch at the subcommittee meeting, I thought back to *Staggerlee* and added, "We'll call it 'Lundi Gras'!" "Call it what?" came the surprised response. "'Lundi Gras,'" I repeated.

Carol Lentz, a Rouse marketing executive, agreed to the idea and became the key person in shaping the staging of the event. The Rex captain was interested but initially expressed some concern. The night belonged to Proteus, he said. Rex would not participate unless Proteus agreed. Proteus not only supported the idea but agreed to the Poydras loop, as well. Planning began.

Another concern of the Rex captain was the type of boat on which the King of Carnival would arrive. It would be inappropriate for Rex to favor any commercial carrier. Instead, the captain secured a neutral ship, a U.S. Coast Guard cutter, thus making the Coast Guard Rex's navy.

A Coast Guard cutter streams out a fountain of water in celebration of the Rex arrival on Lundi Gras. (Photo by Peggy Scott Laborde)

Rex receives a military salute as he arrives at Riverwalk for Lundi Gras festivities.
(Photo © Mitchel Osborne)

The Riverwalk Jazz Band performs for Rex when the monarch arrives on Lundi Gras. (Photo by Peggy Scott Laborde)

The Rex captain, Rex, and emcee Errol Laborde at Lundi Gras festivities. (Photo © Mitchel Osborne)

In 2012, Rex and Mayor Mitch Landrieu press down the plunger to "start" the fireworks display during Lundi Gras festivities. (Photo by Peggy Scott Laborde)

On the evening of Lundi Gras 1987, Rex arrived by cutter at Spanish Plaza and, escorted by a Coast Guard color guard, emerged with his captain, lieutenants, and personal entourage. A huge, good-natured crowd greeted the king. Rex was welcomed onstage by Mayor Sidney Barthelemy. His Honor and His Royalty exchanged proclamations. Rex had pulled a bit of a surprise for the occasion, arriving in a period costume complete with mask, a replica of the king's wardrobe for the 1917 arrival.

Once the proclamations were delivered, Rex and the mayor pushed down a plunger that symbolically detonated fireworks over the river, marking the arrival of the king and Mardi Gras.

After Rex and company left, there was music on the stage until the signal came that Proteus, for the first time turning toward the river, was arriving. A huge second-line moved from the plaza to Poydras, delivering a bounty of revelers to Proteus.

Rex would continue to arrive on Lundi Gras. In future years, the city's diplomatic corps would be in attendance to greet and to be greeted. Amazingly, the fireworks display triggered by Rex and the mayor is the only public pyrotechnics display in all of Carnival.

After a few years, Zulu started staging an arrival, too, an hour earlier, at five o'clock, at the Aquarium of the Americas, downriver from the Rex arrival. Over the years, Zulu would also develop a daylong riverfront music festival. Eventually, the reigning Zulu king and his entourage began visiting Rex after his arrival—a ritual of staggering symbolic importance.

By the time Proteus returned to the parade route in 2000 after a hiatus triggered by the 1992 ordinance controversy, Orpheus also marched along the path, and the riverfront loop was no longer feasible. Still, the crowds at the riverfront waiting to see Rex remained huge.

With each passing year, the term "Lundi Gras" would become more common. The true story behind the origin would be obfuscated, but activity along the river on the day before Mardi Gras was expanding, and the phrase "Lundi Gras" would belong to the ages.

Rex in Modern Times

Besides having the distinction of being the King of Carnival, Rex also presides over the oldest continually parading organization. From the date of his first parade, February 13, 1872, Rex, like Carnival, has marched through good times and bad. Along the way, the King of Carnival has managed to hang on to tradition yet face the present.

To its credit, the Rex School of Design still stages a traditional parade rooted in the nineteenth-century style. The typical structure, with a captain and lieutenants, remains the same. To be selected as Rex is still a high civic honor. At the Rex Room at Antoine's Restaurant, pictures of all the monarchs continue to decorate the walls. (In 2013 one change was necessitated after the *Times-Picayune* reduced its production schedule from seven print issues a week to three. Without there being a printed Monday or Tuesday paper, Rex had to move up announcing its monarchs' identities from Monday evening to Saturday so that they could be pictured in the Sunday newspaper.)

Like Antoine's, Rex demonstrates a loyalty to tradition and Old World grandeur. But just as Antoine's once realized that the time had come to add English to its French menus, Rex has had to make some adjustments. It was one of the first krewes to use the Internet as a way of educating people about its theme. Rex's den was redesigned to make room for a "Rex Mart," where signature items are sold to Rex members and their families to help defray krewe expenses. And at Lundi Gras, Rex now welcomes an annual visit from Zulu. In a gesture of unity, the two monarchs, with the reigning mayor looking on, exchange gifts and good wishes.

In 2012, Rex introduced a new signature float, the "Butterfly King," picking up on a theme from the krewe's 1882 ball. Most notably, though, Rex has developed a philanthropic arm, the Pro Bono Publico Foundation.

Like his subjects, Rex was affected by Katrina, not just in terms of waterlines but in the passion to help with the recovery. The Pro Bono Publico Foundation was established to help the new wave of charter schools and other education-related recovery efforts. By 2013, the group announced it had raised almost two million dollars since its inception. Rex members, including some of the most active leaders in the city, have also been urged to get involved with charter school boards.

In 1872, Rex was founded by a group of civic-minded men largely to help the city recover from Reconstruction. In another century, another group of men is aiding in another recovery. Of all American cities, only in New Orleans can it meaningfully be said, "Long live the king."

Satire Arises from the Ghost of Momus

So many folks were mad at Momus that even the governor had to get involved. He sent a telegram to Washington, D.C., hoping to soothe the frayed feelings.

In 1877, feelings were easily bruised. New Orleans, like the rest of the South, was suffering through the last days of Reconstruction. Carnival time generally provided an uneasy truce, to the extent that the U.S. Army band marched in parades, including Momus's of that year, and both the U.S. Army and U.S. Navy greeted Rex when he arrived by river. But Momus, imp that he was, felt the need to level barbs at the federal occupiers and did so in a parade themed "Hades—A Dream of Momus."

Not since Comus had raked the feds with an 1873 parade titled "Missing Links to Darwin's *Origin of the Species"* had there been such satire in Carnival. In that parade, President Grant had been depicted as an insect—a tobacco grub—and Union general Benjamin Butler was shown as a hyena.

Grant was spoofed in the Momus parade, too—portrayed as the devil Beelzebub sitting on an imperial throne. The local agents of federal forces were also teased, including General Butler, who, along with Republican bosses, was displayed standing on a ship sinking into a sea of fire.

Momus marched. Tempers rose. On the next day, there were demands for punishment. Perry Young, in his book, *The Mistick Krewe: Chronicles of Comus and His Kin*, reported that the masker "who impersonated Beelzebub was told to his face that whoever travestied President Grant would be shot if identified."

Gov. Francis T. Nicholls, no supporter of the occupiers but worried that their outrage would increase tensions, fired off a telegram to the state's military representative in Washington, stating, "The sentiment of the whole community is opposed to what happened at the celebration on Thursday."

Nicholls was diplomatic but wrong. Far from being opposed, much of the community was privately giggling. Even the Union general Galusha Pennypacker seemed less offended than others on his side and allowed the infantry to escort Rex on his arrival the following Monday.

Still, the seething continued. A Reconstruction publication called *The Official Journal of the State of Louisiana* complained about the parade and stated that it "is rumored that this is to be the last public display of Momus." It added, "We hope so out of respect for its dead fame."

There was a bit of truth to the rumor. Momus survived, but satire did not. The dream of Hades turned out to be a nightmare. By informal understanding, krewes retreated to the other side of the controversy line. Satire—so naturally a part of any Carnival—was lost in New Orleans for 100 years.

Then in 1977, the Knights of Momus surprised the city by bringing back the barb. There was a contemporary cast of characters to ridicule. In a new age of Carnival with superkrewes and towering floats, Momus was in danger of appearing to be a tired old parade. The return to the barb recharged the group. Momus became a must-see for parade buffs, as a satirical message accompanying the king on his float set the tone for what was to follow. Typical of the Knights' parade was the 1991 march, which poked fun at a high-rolling Edwin Edwards and a befuddled Saddam Hussein. No one knew at the time that the laughing would soon stop.

Momus never paraded again after that year, having retreated once more, this time in the face of a controversial city anti-discrimination ordinance. The floats remained stored in the den, with the satirical images subject to cobwebs. But like the seeds from an aging tree that are carried by the wind and dropped on fertile soil, the Momus spirit was sprouting anew.

First came an unlikely shoot, a Jefferson Parish transplant krewe known as Saturn that redefined itself after having secured a slot on St. Charles Avenue, Carnival's Broadway. Saturn developed a Momus look and a satirical wit sometimes as wicked as vintage Momus. Unfortunately, like Momus, it did not last; in its case the Beelzebub was money.

In 1997, a new group formed, Le Krewe d'Etat, an organization so intent on satire that even its name was a devious pun. In 2001, women participated in Carnival satire for the first time when a popular group called Muses took to the streets. Its barb was sharp. Also debuting in 2001 were the Knights of Chaos, a

The satirical Krewe du Vieux parade features many mule-drawn floats. (Photo ©
Mitchel Osborne)

group that had secured the use of the old Momus floats and took much of the
old krewe's look and character.

So now the number of satirical parades has gone from one to none to one
to three and more—the most ever. (The *Animal House*-like Krewe of Tucks is a
confederation of different group floats all tending to poke fun at life in general,
and the teasing gets rowdy and often off-color when the Krewe du Vieux winds
its way through the Marigny and French Quarter.) The ghost of Momus survives.

Unfortunately, too many parade-goers may not see the ghost for the beads. In
the old days, throws were occasional and sparse; the emphasis was on the design
of the floats. Today the obsession is with catching as much as possible. In a true
setback, krewes have even been rated not by the quality of their float designs but
by the quantity of their throws.

Satirists will be challenged to deliver their punch lines through the seas of
waving arms. But topical humor may be the way to make people pay more
attention to floats as an art form. Bringing wit back to Carnival: that would truly
be a dream of Momus.

The Society of St. Anne Captures the Spirit

At Carnival, it is the masquerade that makes the moment, not the unmasked.
Nowhere is it written that the season is to be expressed solely by throwing trinkets
from floats. Go to the streets of Bywater and Faubourg Marigny on Mardi Gras

Members of the Society of St. Anne, a group that marches through the Bywater, Marigny, and French Quarter neighborhoods on Carnival Day, are known for their elaborate and colorful costumes. (Photo © Mitchel Osborne)

morning, and experience the moment as the spirits intended.

Stand at the corner of Royal and Kerlerec streets, and let the pageantry pass before you. At some point, spilling from the back streets of the neighborhood will come maskers, hundreds—perhaps thousands—of them, with an occasional band blended into the procession. You are witnessing the passing of the Society of St. Anne, a gathering of free spirits festooned in creative masquerade. They rest alongside the R Bar in their migration toward the French Quarter and then Canal Street, where those who survive the journey will see the King of Carnival and his parade.

It is when St. Anne is moving through the Quarter, up the heralded Rue Royal, that this flock is at its sensory richest, with all its colors and quirkiness funneled into one channel. Those standing on the stoops watching the procession are experiencing the soul of the season. There are other groups blended in, including the Society of St. Anthony, and somewhere in the flock there will be the Ducks of Dixieland and the Krewe of Cosmic Debris. The totality, though, is joined together under the banner of St. Anne; it's a group that any saint who admires rituals would appreciate.

St. Anne was founded in 1969, but for many of its early years, it was mostly a Marigny event. It would be hard to pinpoint the exact

A reveler from the Society of St. Anne. (Photo © Mitchel Osborne)

Opposite and above: *Maskers from the Society of St. Anne.* (Photos © Mitchel Osborne)

Members of the Society of St. Anne. (Photo by Peggy Scott Laborde)

New Orleans actress Becky Allen during the Mardi Gras Day procession of the Society of St. Anne. (Photo by Peggy Scott Laborde)

Society of St. Anne member. (Photo © Mitchel Osborne)

Dancing in the streets is a common sight on Mardi Gras Day. (Photo by Peggy Scott Laborde)

moment of its flowering, and there have been schisms and disagreements through the years, but certainly aficionados have been flocking to the procession with increased fervor since the late eighties. Pity those who think they have experienced Mardi Gras without ever having felt the energy of the Society of Saint Anne passing by. They might as well be in Mobile.

Subkrewes : A New Generation

Walking groups have long been a part of Carnival. The Jefferson City Buzzards, the Lyons, and the Corner Club have made an annual trek down St. Charles Avenue on Mardi Gras. Other groups, including the Ducks of Dixieland and the Krewe of Cosmic Debris, patrol Marigny and the French Quarter on Mardi Gras. The Ducks also take part in the Tucks parade, and the Buzzards cross the parish line to participate in the Metairie St. Patrick's Day parade. The Krewe du Vieux, which marches on the Saturday before the regular parade season begins, is really a collection of individual groups, such as the Krewe of Underwear, that parade under a common theme.

Mondo Kayo, a group with a Caribbean theme, adds a lot of flash and energy as it sashays up St. Charles on Mardi Gras and then settles on Frenchmen Street for more dancing.

Muses opened the way for more groups to come into existence. The Rolling Elvi, Bearded Oysters, Camel Toe Lady Steppers, and Ninth Ward Marching Band are regulars in their parades. Another female group, the Muff-A-Lottas, works out its own dance routine, and each marcher takes on a character name, including one whose red wig allows her to be "Ruby Red."

Most famous of the new groups is the all-guy 610 Stompers, who, in 2011, even dazzled the crowd—and confused the TV announcers—at the Macy's Thanksgiving Day Parade in New York (as though they had never seen beefy guys in hot pants dancing in the streets). The Stompers' origin traces back not to Mardi Gras but to the parade held in honor of the late sports-radio talk-show host Buddy Diliberto in the year when the Saints went to the Super Bowl. (The parade was to honor Diliberto's

The Jefferson City Buzzards, founded in 1890, parade in front of Gallier Hall on Mardi Gras 1965. (Photo courtesy of Richard Hofler and the Jefferson City Buzzards)

Some Jefferson City Buzzards outside Franky & Johnny's Restaurant, where they were traditionally greeted by the Phunny Phorty Phellows. (Photo by Peggy Scott Laborde)

The Ducks of Dixieland, a New Orleans walking club that debuted in 1985, costume in a different theme each year. (Photo © Mitchel Osborne)

Opposite: *Note the fleur-de-lis symbol so beloved by locals on the dress of this Society of St Anne reveler. (Photo © Mitchel Osborne)*

promise that if the Saints ever made it to the big game, he would wear a dress.) Carnival has created more opportunities for the Stompers to strut.

What is good about these groups is that they bring humor to the parade route. They are another way for people to participate in Carnival without having to spend a bundle on beads.

Subkrewes are also showing up in other parades, including Le Krewe d'Etat and Tucks, a practice that other krewes would do well to follow.

For the groups, the future is unlimited. For the Rolling Elvi, in which men dressed in various interpretations of "The King" ride motorized scooters, there is even a female auxiliary whose members follow the group in a truck. Their name: the Priscillas.

STORIES TOLD

Anniversary Confusions

Suppose you started a new job in February of a certain year. When then should you celebrate your first anniversary? A reasonable answer would be February a year later. But if you use Carnival time, you should have celebrated your first year on your first day on the job.

That is part of the confusion that Carnival faces in presenting its anniversaries. Do you measure something from the first time something happened? Or do you measure it from one year later, as we do in celebrating birthdays and special occasions? A married couple, for example, celebrates its first anniversary a year after the wedding and not on the day of the ceremony.

In Carnival, depending on who is doing the celebrating, the calculations go both ways. The old-line organizations tend to favor the former method. Thus Rex, which first paraded in 1872, celebrated its centennial in 1971. Zulu, on the other hand, which bases its anniversary on the year that it was incorporated (1909), celebrated its 100th anniversary in 2009. Had it done it the Rex way, the centennial would have been a year earlier.

For mediation we call on a higher authority, namely the Louisiana State Lottery, which in 2009 printed scratch-off tickets to commemorate the fiftieth anniversary of Al Johnson's R&B song "Carnival Time." The state's calculations were based on early recordings being made in 1959, so, in a non-Rex manner, 2009 was the fiftieth anniversary.

Rex, however, in 2009 stuck to its method in celebrating the fiftieth anniversary of parade doubloons, which were first tossed from its floats in 1960. By some ways of counting, 2010 would be the fiftieth, but that's not the Rex way.

King Sargon, the signature name for each year's king of the Knights of Babylon, presented an opportunity for Solomon-like wisdom in determining the Knights' seventieth anniversary, which was also being celebrated in 2009. The anniversary could be based on 1939, the year when the Jester's Club, Babylon's parent organization, was founded, or on 1940, the year of the first parade. Take your pick.

Among the many Carnival Day walking clubs is Mondo Kayo. Its members wear Caribbean-inspired costumes. (Photo by Peggy Scott Laborde)

Spotting brilliantly costumed walking groups such as St. Cecilia is a highlight of Carnival Day. (Photo © Mitchel Osborne)

The 610 Stompers perform in the Muses parade. The group is named after an upper-deck seating section in the Superdome. (Photo © Mitchel Osborne)

I propose standardization of the way anniversaries are determined, although I am not sure who should do the standardizing. If I were emperor, reigning over all these kings, I would demand the year-later method. Under my dictum, Zulu would have been 100 in 2009, but Rex's bicentennial would be in 2072 not '71. But then again, the King of Carnival, I suppose, rules supreme.

Meanwhile, those of you who have read this far are invited back next year when the first anniversary of reading this is celebrated. Or should it be today?

Carnival Day: A Personal Experience

Every Mardi Gras, I walk from Canal Street to Frenchmen Street and then back again. That seems sane enough, except that I probably make the round trip, with deviations to Bourbon Street and Jackson Square, maybe five times. I am obsessed. I have to see it all.

Were it not for Rex, I probably would not make it to Canal Street, but I always have to pay proper deference to Carnival's classiest parade. But then it's back into the Quarter and the mystery of Marigny for more discovery. Memories from 2011 included a shout-off between Christian fundamentalists saying that we're all going to hell and activist Leo Watermeier yelling back. The scene, which has gone on for years now, is both amusing and maddening. All have their right to speak, but come on, it's Mardi Gras. Couldn't we save the damnation for Ash Wednesday?

Skin and the showing of it are very much a part of the scene and always have been dating back to the pagan rites of spring, when people would frolic naked in the fields and orgies were part of the Saturnalia's agenda. Is someone

The Krewe of the Rolling Elvi are a welcome sight in the Muses parade. The members wear costumes based on Elvis Presley's career and ride motorized scooters. (Photo © Mitchel Osborne)

Coleen Salley, a longtime University of New Orleans professor and children's-book author, led the Krewe of Coleen around the French Quarter for many years. (Photo by Peggy Scott Laborde)

The 'Tit Rǝx parade, started by Jeremy Yuslum, is a procession of shoebox floats that rolls through the Bywater and Marigny neighborhoods. This "Wrecks" king's float was made by Jeannie Detweiler and Susan Dunlap. (Photo by Nancy Bernardo)

Dogs are royalty in the Krewe of Barkus. (Photo © Mitchel Osborne)

topless if the top is painted? I'm not sure. That may be for the courts, or the fundamentalists, to decide.

Even by Mardi Gras standards, every so often something hits me as being especially funny. In 2011, it was the Tin Man at an ATM. Here we have the yin and yang of technology: the Tin Man having to remove his top in order to reach his debit card.

I was just about to surrender for the evening when something told me to take one more stroll down Chartres Street. I am glad I did. In the distance, I saw the Preservation Hall Jazz Band approaching. Leading the impromptu parade as grand marshal was bluegrass star Del McCoury. His group and the hall's band have performed together several times, creating a real fusion of Southern roots

The Children's Carnival Club has been staging balls since the 1920s. (Photo © Mitchel Osborne)

Bluegrass star Del McCoury was a grand marshal for he Preservation Hall Jazz Band on Mardi Gras 2012. (Photo by Errol Laborde)

music. I am not sure if McCoury understood all that was going on, but one thing was clear: he wasn't in the Virginia hills anymore.

I walked so much that that night I was awakened by a cramp in one leg, which somehow spread to the other so that I had two charley horses working simultaneously. I was in so much pain for a few minutes that all I could do was stare at the ceiling—and wonder if I was missing anything on Frenchmen Street.

EPILOGUE 1

The Quintessential Carnival

I once had a conversation with a man who was an official of the Knights of Hermes. He was effusive about the group's upcoming parade. "It will be the most beautiful ever!" he exclaimed. He also mentioned the parade's theme, which was one of those obscure classical legends that only two people along the parade route, if that many, would be familiar with, but I respected that. As the man continued,

The Krewe of Hermes king's float. (Photo © Mitchel Osborne)

Mayor deLesseps S. Morrison presents Queen Ethel Elizabeth Seiler at the Krewe of Hermes Ball in the Municipal Auditorium, February 22, 1952. (Photo by Leon Trice Photography, courtesy of the Louisiana Division/City Archives, New Orleans Public Library)

I thought that here was an example of the best of Mardi Gras. First there was a theme that hearkened back to the days when classically educated men drew from mythology and history to design their parades rather than pandering to the crowds, and then there was the creativity of designing floats to fit the theme. Hermes is one of the groups that does things well, rather than presenting some makeshift, off-the-lot parade, with rented floats ridiculously forced into a generic theme.

That got me to thinking about what might be called the "quintessential" Mardi Gras, those parts of Carnival life that reflect quality and tradition, are not about commercialism, and are enduring. Most of what is quintessential is lost the farther one gets from New Orleans, but in the city the roses still grow, even among the weeds.

Here, then, is my list.

Original Floats with Esoteric Themes

Comus began it all but no longer parades. Following in the tradition are Rex, Proteus, Hermes, Babylon, and, among the superkrewes, Orpheus.

Original Floats with Satirical Themes

Momus and Comus both fooled with satire back in the politically touchy days of Reconstruction. Momus, who reintroduced the barb in 1977, remains in his den (Carnival speak for no longer parading), but carrying on the tradition are Chaos, Muses, and Le Krewe d'Etat.

Jefferson City Buzzards

This group has been around since 1890, sashaying down St. Charles Avenue on Mardi Gras morning. Other marching groups have emerged since, but the Buzzards, who have their own Uptown clubhouse, came first.

177

A float from the Hermes parade. (Photo © Mitchel Osborne)

The king's float of the Krewe of Proteus. (Photo © Mitchel Osborne)

The Krewe of Proteus, which first paraded in 1882, still uses wooden cotton wagons for its floats. (Photo © Mitchel Osborne)

A Trojan horse was part of one local marching group's presentation on Carnival Day. (Photo by Errol Laborde)

R&B Carnival Songs

Mardi Gras has inspired music in many genres, including jazz, country (the original version of "Mardi Gras Mambo"), Cajun, and more. But it's the R&B songs that are played over and over every year. They are like robins, whose appearance is a harbinger of the new season. Professor Longhair's "Go to the Mardi Gras" has that impossible-to-keep-still-to beat; the Nevilles-ish Hawketts' version of "Mambo" put Gert Town on the map; and the staccato blasts at the beginning of Al Johnson's "Carnival Time" introduce Carnival's liveliest tune, albeit one that talks about a barroom fire on Mardi Gras. Who cares? It's Carnival time!

Marine Corps Band New Orleans

There is no sharper band in all of Carnival than the local Marine Corps Band. The musicianship and movements are perfect, both in the parades and at the balls.

Society of St. Anne

Carnival's greatest confederation of mixed maskers ascends from the streets of Bywater and Marigny and then crosses the Quarter toward Canal Street, providing a procession that totally captures the spirit of the season.

Lundi Gras

"Lundi Gras" has become part of the common language of Carnival since Rex restarted his annual tradition of arriving by boat. There is still majesty in seeing a king arrive. Lately Zulu has visited him—and the partying begins.

Mardi Gras Indians, in the Neighborhoods

A once very isolated practice got national attention with the HBO series "Treme," whose storylines included the post-Katrina plight of a Mardi Gras Indian chief. The New Orleans tribes are certainly worthy of sociological attention, but we appreciate that they also cling to their neighborhood roots. In the streets of Uptown and the Seventh Ward, they provide feathery flashes unlike anything else seen in Carnival.

Jock-A-Mo-Fee-Na-Ne

Something that is culturally rich even has elements of its own language. If you don't understand what the big chief says, then "jock-a-mo-fee-na-ne" to you.

Signature Floats

All of the really good parades have original floats built around a creative theme, but dispersed throughout those parades are krewe signature floats—those that are a part of the krewe's annual appearance. Following are some of my favorite examples.

Rex: His Majesty's Royal Bandwagon; Butterfly King
Bacchus: Bacchawhoppa
Endymion: Ol' Man River; Pontchartrain Beach, Then and Now
Orpheus: Leviathan; Trojan Horse

Among the "throne floats" (those that the monarch rides), Proteus's with the sea-god theme is one of the most magical.

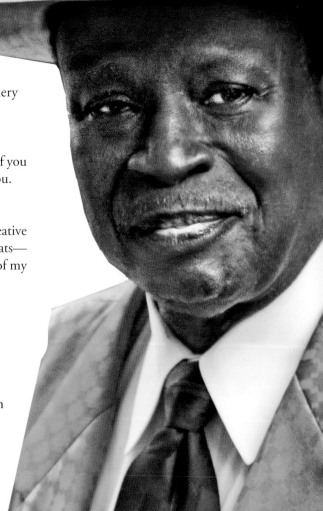

Al Johnson's 1960 "Carnival Time" is a Mardi Gras rhythm and blues classic. (Photo © Judi Bottoni)

The 2013 Mardi Gras season saw the debut of an Endymion float celebrating the history of the beloved Pontchartrain Beach Amusement Park. The Zephyr was the wooden rollercoaster. (Photo © Mitchel Osborne)

Over a million dollars was spent on the Pontchartrain Beach float in the Endymion parade. (Photo © Mitchel Osborne)

Muses Walking Groups

Just as Rex, when it staged its first parade in 1872, allowed more participation from "miscellaneous" maskers, Muses has created the opportunity for new and creative groups to take to the streets. Some of the freshest participants in Carnival are marching between the floats in Muses.

Rex Mounted Lieutenants

Dressed in waves of purple, green, and gold, these masked riders are among Mardi Gras morning's most striking sights.

Gay Carnival Balls

Though gay creativity permeates all of Carnival, the most visual manifestation is the gay Carnival balls. No one does it with more grandeur, and feathers, than these groups.

Petronius

Self-described as the "grande dame" of gay Mardi Gras, this krewe has moved into its second half-century. It is to gay Carnival balls what Comus was to establishing parades and traditions. Much of what was to follow was shaped and influenced by the earlier group.

St. Charles Avenue During a Parade

With the canopy of oaks, the wide neutral ground, and the charm of the surroundings, there is no better place in the world for watching a Mardi Gras parade. Snared beads dangling from the trees throughout the year provide testimony that this is the favored route of Carnival's march.

"If Ever I Cease to Love"

What began as a nineteenth-century burlesque song has been modified into marches, waltzes, jazz, and more, and the lyrics have taken on new meanings. Yet Carnival's anthem works both as something that is easy to dance to and that can accompany a royal procession. Is there a better Carnival song? If so, may the Grand Duke Alexis ride a buffalo through Texas.

Purple, Green, and Gold

Initially devised by Rex from the laws of heraldry, the colors are a perfect blend that is both royal and celebratory. Plus, no other sovereign has the same tricolors.

Rex/Comus Ball

In the beginning there was Comus, creator of traditions, and then came Rex, the people's monarch. At the end of each Carnival season, the people symbolically bow to tradition, and in the world of Carnival, that's how it should be,

Flambeaux

Once near extinction, new ones have been created by Le Krewe d'Etat and Orpheus, to go along with the vintage torches owned by Proteus. The glow

Rex mounted lieutenants display the Carnival colors during the parade. (Photo © Mitchel Osborne)

This young reveler shares her beads while she and her family wait for the parades on St. Charles Avenue on Mardi Gras Day. (Photo by Morgan Packard)

A family on Mardi Gras Day. (Photo by Peggy Scott Laborde)

This tiny masker has her very own spaceship. (Photo by Peggy Scott Laborde)

Families in costume are a welcome sight on Mardi Gras Day.
(Photo © Mitchel Osborne)

of the lights creates a golden hue ideal for illuminating floats and visually returning the moment to antiquity.

Bordeaux Street Float Den

What secrets remain there? Do the dusty remains of the former Comus and Momus parades still stand? Is there life among the Chaos? Mystery will always be a quintessential element of Carnival.

EPILOGUE 2

Stir Me Something, Mister

If Carnival is supposed to represent a farewell to feasting, first comes the feasting part. With the help of some fine chefs and cookbook authors, I've assembled recipes for a few favorites of the season. First, though, let's examine Carnival's greatest food hits.

SIXTEEN TOP FOODS OF THE LOUISIANA MARDI GRAS

The Krewe of Cork, with perennial king Patrick Van Hoorebeek, left, is comprised of many members of the local restaurant industry. (Photo © Mitchel Osborne)

Carnival has never been about fine dining but more about party food or munching on the go. Vendors offer the standard fare found most anyplace; far better are those items that really reflect the state and its Carnival. Here (in alphabetical order) is my list of the top Louisiana Mardi Gras foods.

Barbecue

Location: Along parade routes throughout the state.
Advantage: Smoking grill provides a picnic setting at the parade.
Disadvantage: Sometimes messy cleanup after the parade. Moving the grill may require a truck. Also, smoke sometimes bothers the rest of the crowd.
Comment: There's a place somewhere to the west of Louisiana called Texas where barbecuing consists of pork or beef. They don't barbecue chicken over there, perhaps because they don't have Mardi Gras parades to wait for, so they can take their time. Chicken cooks faster, and since the coals don't need to be lit before dawn, it is perfect for parade preparation. Sauce is optional.

Boudin

Location: Along parade routes in Lake Charles, Lafayette, and Acadiana and as far north as New Roads.
Advantage: Portability and packaging. Can be eaten like a hot dog.
Disadvantage: Sometimes the stuffing squirts out when chomped into. Eat with caution.
Comment: We're talking about the so-called "white boudin," not "black

185

Food stands become a familiar sight in Downtown New Orleans during the Carnival season. (Photo © Mitchel Osborne)

boudin," which is blood sausage and best served to the vampires in your party.

Cochon de Lait (Suckling Pig)

Location: Cajun Country and up into Central Louisiana.

Advantage: As though planned by nature, Carnival season is also near the time of the winter *boucheries* ("cookouts"), so the meat is not long off the hog. Roasting fires can heat up cold February days.

Disadvantage: Roasting a suckling pig is not really something you can do along a parade route; it's better for before or after the parade.

Comment: Boucheries also provide auxiliary products such as hogshead cheese, sausage, and (see below) cracklins.

Cracklins (aka *Gratons*)

Location: Throughout the state, though not so much in the New Orleans area.

Advantage: Easy to snack on before a parade.

Disadvantage: Deep-fried, salted pork skin can never be confused with health food.

Opposite: *This reveler redefines the term "moveable feast."* (Photo © Mitchel Osborne)

Some locals have a picnic while waiting for parades. (Photo © Mitchel Osborne)

Comment: While I would not recommend eating them every day, perfectly prepared cracklins provide a bouquet of flavors in which the saltiness from the skin combines with the sweetness of the meat, both enhanced by the crunchiness of the bite.

Crawfish

Location: Backyard parties throughout the state.

Advantage: Knowing how to peel them is a good way of separating the locals from the Yankees. Tossing potatoes, onions, garlic, and sausage into the pot can add to the feast.

Disadvantage: Seasonal availability may fluctuate. Since mudbugs are not yet in their prime during Carnival time, they may be a bit small.

Comment: Sucking the heads is not only appropriate but should be required by law so as not to waste the full flavor of the crawfish.

Dirty Rice

Location: Mostly in rural and Cajun prairie areas; also anywhere where there are Popeyes Chicken outlets, which is most everywhere.

Advantage: Makes a convenient rice dish that combines organ meats with spices.

Disadvantage: Combines organ meats with spices.

Comment: The dish's name has become commonly Americanized to "rice dressing." Popeyes does some dishes very well (see fried chicken below); dirty rice, which is referred to on the menu as "Cajun rice," is not one of them. Best versions are found on home stoves.

Etouffée

Location: At parade parties, primarily in French Louisiana.

Advantage: Provides a good hearty "smothered" dish cooked in a pot and made with shrimp or crawfish, tomatoes, and seasonings ladled over rice.

Disadvantage: It's hard to bring the pot to the parade, especially if it is cast iron.

Comment: This is an ultimate Louisiana dish combining local seafood and, most likely, homegrown rice. Consider it your patriotic duty to go for seconds.

Fried Chicken

Location: Throughout the state, along parade routes, even discreetly on some floats.

Advantage: Classic parade food; easy portability.

Disadvantage: Greasy fingers could cause beads to slip through.

Comment: Popeyes, which originated in New Orleans, not only provides the best commercial fried chicken but also has set the standard for other chicken outlets. Done at home, remember that frying chicken correctly takes time, so plan accordingly.

Grillades and Grits

Location: After the ball at late-night krewe breakfasts in New Orleans.

Advantage: Provides a good, flavorful late-night meal with a Southern touch.

Disadvantage: Buffet plates must be handled carefully to avoid spilling on evening dresses or tuxedoes.

Comment: Grillades can vary; most often they are veal, pork, or beef served in a gravy. Grits can be hit or miss. Butter helps.

Gumbo

Location: In Cajun Country, especially in homes along the route of the Courir de Mardi Gras.

Advantage: When done well, it can be a several-course meal in one bowl.

Disadvantage: Varies considerably in quality from place to place. Depends highly on individual roux-making skills.

Comment: There are many variations, but for Mardi Gras we are talking about chicken-and-sausage gumbo. This and king cake are the only foods that are part of Mardi Gras rituals. Riders in the Courir de Mardi Gras steer their steeds from house to house to "steal" gumbo ingredients.

Jambalaya

Location: Statewide, mostly at parties.

Advantage: Mass quantities can be produced inexpensively and served hot.

Disadvantage: When done right, it can be excellent, but when diluted just to feed the masses, it can be bland. In that case, just pick away at the sausage fragments.

Comments: Like gumbo, variations can feature either chicken and sausage or seafood (mostly shrimp). For chilly parade-going days, the meat versions are heartier.

King Cake

Location: Once exclusive to New Orleans, they are now made by bakeries throughout the state.

Advantage: This is Carnival's most indigenous food and the only confection linked directly to Mardi Gras. Complements any occasion.

Disadvantage: Lots of sugar.

Comment: King cakes are experiencing their golden age, now that bakers are injecting the confections with various flavored fillings. No longer are king cakes a tasteless brioche; they have become a flavor explosion. If you get the plastic baby in your slice, the protocol is to admit it and buy the king cake for the next gathering. At the New Orleans society ball of the Twelfth Night Revelers, the queen is symbolically selected by getting the slice with a gold bean in it.

MoonPie®

Location: Along parade routes after being tossed from floats.

Advantage: Arrives safely wrapped in cellophane. For those who need it, can provide a quick sugar jolt.

Disadvantage: Frequently placed with other parade catches, getting squished in the process.

Comment: MoonPies® are the Mobile Mardi Gras's (via Chattanooga) gift to the nation's Carnival. The circular pies have just the right heft to be thrown from a float. In some places it is illegal for riders to toss food, but MoonPies®, because they are packaged, usually win the law's approval.

Potato Salad

Location: In North Louisiana as a side dish with barbecue; in South Louisiana as an accompaniment to gumbo.

Advantage: Great versatility, including many styles, textures, and flavors. (I like it smooth with egg, bacon, mayonnaise, mustard, and—yes—apple.)

Disadvantage: Not strictly a Louisiana dish but goes well with Louisiana foods. Sometimes gets overlooked on the serving table.

Comment: In some parts of Acadiana, most notably St. Martin Parish, gumbo is often served over potato salad, rather than rice.

Red Beans and Rice

Location: New Orleans area.

Advantage: Beans are a healthy food, and sausage and/or pickled meat add a jolt of flavor. Warm, lightly salted rice can be soothing.

Disadvantage: Not as versatile as jambalaya, another rice dish, in terms of ingredients. (You never hear of red beans and shrimp, though someone should try it.)

Comment: This is the only dish with a day of the week associated with it: Monday. In New Orleans, red beans and rice is the traditional lunch for that day. With the emergence of the Lundi Gras celebration, the dish is ideal for that day.

Sweet Potato

Location: Southern, Central, and North Louisiana, most often as a side dish for gumbo.

Advantage: Rich in protein, iron, calcium, vitamins A and C, plus complex carbohydrates, the sweet potato is one of the healthiest of all foods.

Disadvantage: There is none.

Comment: Baked in an oven, it develops a caramelized fragrance that makes you glad to be in the kitchen. I agree with those who plop the tuber in their gumbo bowl and use its sweet taste to counterbalance the gumbo's spiciness.

RECIPES FOR THE SEASON

Grillades and Grits
Chef Lazone Randolph
Brennan's

Executive Chef Lazone Randolph has worked at Brennan's since the 1960s, following in the footsteps of Chefs Paul Blangé and Mike Roussel. He shares

Grits and grillades from Brennan's. (Photo by Cheryl Gerber; courtesy of Brennan's)

Lazone Randolph is the executive chef of Brennan's. (Courtesy of Brennan's)

here a time-honored dish that is especially popular at breakfasts that take place at several New Orleans Carnival balls.

Chef Lazone has appeared on the Food Network, Travel Channel, local morning shows, and public-television station WYES-TV.

GRILLADES
8 thinly pounded veal escalopes, about 3 oz. each
Salt and black pepper
½ cup (1 stick) butter (olive oil can be substituted)
½ cup olive oil
½ cup chopped onions
½ cup chopped green onions
3 garlic cloves, finely chopped
1½ cups chopped green bell pepper
½ cup chopped celery
1 bay leaf
1½ tsp. Italian seasoning
4 ripe tomatoes, diced
1 tbsp. Worcestershire sauce
2 tbsp. tomato paste
1 qt. beef stock
2 tbsp. cornstarch
¼ cup water
2 tbsp. chopped fresh parsley
Plantation Grits (see below)

Preheat oven to 175 degrees.

Season the veal escalopes on both sides with salt and pepper. Heat the butter in a large skillet and sauté the veal until lightly browned, about 3 minutes per side. Transfer the cooked meat to a platter and place in the warm oven while preparing the sauce.

Heat the olive oil in a large saucepan, then sauté the onions, green onions, garlic, bell pepper, and celery in the hot oil until tender. Stir in the bay leaf, Italian seasoning, tomatoes, Worcestershire, and tomato paste. When the mixture is well blended, add the beef stock and cook for 5 minutes, stirring frequently.

In a small bowl, blend the cornstarch with ¼ cup water. Stir the liquid cornstarch into the sauce, then add the parsley. Season with salt and pepper to taste and cook over medium-high heat until the sauce is reduced by about one-fourth. Before serving, remove the bay leaf.

PLANTATION GRITS
5 cups water
1 tsp. salt
1 cup uncooked grits
¼ cup (½ stick) butter

In a medium saucepan, bring water to a boil along with the salt. Gradually add the grits to the pan, stirring constantly. Reduce the heat and simmer the grits until thickened, 5 to 10 minutes. Add the butter and stir until the butter is melted throughout.

To serve the dish, spoon grillade sauce onto 8 plates and center a veal escalope on each. Place cooked grits on the side of the meat, ladle additional sauce over the veal and grits, and serve.

Serves 8.

Chicken and Andouille Gumbo
Chef Jeremy Langlois
Latil's Landing Restaurant, Houmas House Plantation

Chef Jeremy Langlois began his culinary career the day after his sixteenth birthday in May of 1995, when he joined Chef John Folse's White Oak Plantation team. Within seven months, he was promoted to prep cook. Seeing the enthusiasm and potential in his young protégé, Chef Folse gave him a full scholarship to the Chef John Folse Culinary Institute at Nicholls State University.

In 2001, at the age of twenty-two, Chef Langlois was promoted to executive chef at the award-winning Lafitte's Landing Restaurant at Bittersweet Plantation. Today he leads the culinary team at Houmas House Plantation as executive chef of the award-winning Latil's Landing Restaurant, named by *Esquire Magazine* in 2005 as one of the top twenty best new restaurants in America. There he masterfully creates wonderful dishes in a style that he calls "Nouvelle Louisiane."

Jeremy Langlois is the executive chef at Latil's Landing Restaurant at Houmas House Plantation. (Courtesy of Houmas House Plantation)

½ lb. andouille sausage, cut into ¼-in. slices
8 tbsp. vegetable oil, divided
1 2½- to 3-lb. chicken, cut into pieces

Chef Jeremy Langlois's Chicken and Andouille Gumbo. (Photo by Jeremy Langlois)

1½ qt. water
½ cup all-purpose flour
1 cup chopped onions
1 cup chopped celery
1 cup chopped green bell pepper
2 garlic cloves, finely chopped
2 tbsp. chopped fresh parsley
2 bay leaves
½ tsp. chopped thyme
1 tsp. Louisiana hot sauce
Salt and black pepper to taste
½ cup chopped green onions
Cooked rice

In a 3-qt. Dutch oven, over medium-high heat, brown the sausage in 4 tbsp. oil, about 7 minutes. Remove with slotted spoon and set aside. Add chicken pieces and cook until golden brown, about 10 minutes, turning occasionally.

Add water, cover, and cook until chicken is tender, about 30 minutes. Remove chicken, leaving liquid in pan, and when chicken is cool enough to handle, discard skin and bones and dice meat into ½-in. cubes.

In another 3-qt. Dutch oven, over medium heat, mix remaining 4 tbsp. oil and flour and cook, stirring constantly, until roux turns dark brown, about 30 minutes. Add onions, celery, bell pepper, garlic, and parsley and cook about 10 minutes or until vegetables are tender. Add the liquid used to cook the chicken, along with the bay leaves, thyme, hot sauce, salt, and pepper. Bring to a boil, reduce heat, and simmer, uncovered, 45 minutes. Add chicken and sausage and simmer another 15 minutes.

Remove pan from heat, add green onions, and adjust seasoning. To serve, mound rice in each soup bowl, then ladle gumbo around rice.

Serves 12.

Mardi Gras Morning Deviled Eggs
Poppy Tooker
Radio host, cooking-school teacher, and cookbook author

Cookbook author and radio-show host/producer Poppy Tooker. (Courtesy of Poppy Tooker)

Poppy Tooker is the host/producer of the NPR-affiliated weekly radio show "Louisiana Eats!" She contributes colorful food commentary on "Steppin' Out," the New Orleans PBS affiliate's weekly arts and entertainment program on WYES. She has shared the screen with television celebrities such as "Extreme Cuisine"'s Jeff Corwin and "Foodography"'s Mo Rocca, and even Bobby Flay could not resist challenging Poppy to a throwdown. Her famous seafood gumbo proved unbeatable on his popular Food Network show!

In 1999, Poppy brought the international Slow Food movement to New Orleans by founding the local chapter, one of the first in the United States. An award-winning cookbook author, she wrote the foreword for and added updated recipes to Pelican Publishing Company's *Mme. Bégué's Recipes of Old New Orleans Creole Cookery*, first published in 1900.

About her deviled egg recipe, she says, "You'll want to collect some washed, empty egg cartons to bring dozens of these delicious eggs out on the parade route. Also, stick a toothpick in each carton to help lift them out of the carton when serving on the neutral ground!"

6 hardboiled eggs
2 tbsp. butter, softened
½ tsp. Creole mustard
1 tbsp. finely diced tasso or ham
1 green onion, finely minced
Salt and hot sauce to taste
Paprika

Peel eggs and cut in half crosswise instead of lengthwise as usual. (This way the deviled eggs will fit into the egg cartons for easy transportation.) Remove yolks and mash together with the softened butter and Creole mustard. Mix in tasso and green onion, then season with salt and hot sauce to taste.

Put stuffing in a pastry bag, or put in a plastic zip-type bag and cut off one bottom corner. Pipe filling into egg halves and place into egg carton. Garnish with a sprinkle of paprika. Refrigerate eggs, but when serving them, allow to come to room temperature again.

Serves 6–12.

Milk Punch
Poppy Tooker

Poppy says, "This is de rigueur for Mardi Gras morning on the St. Charles Avenue neutral ground as we wait for Rex. I mix it up the night before by the plastic, gallon-milk jug size, so they are ready in the ice chest. Shake well before pouring into go-cups for toasting.

"One Mardi Gras morning, friends with small children who'd spent Lundi Gras night with us were up especially early. I walked into the kitchen to find the kids protesting their bowls of breakfast cereal, complaining, 'Mom, there's something wrong with this milk!' That's because 'Mom' had unknowingly doused their Cheerios with milk punch instead of just plain milk!"

1 cup (8 oz.) brandy or bourbon
2¼ cups half-and-half
¼ tsp. vanilla extract
3 tbsp. powdered sugar
Fresh grated nutmeg

Mix all ingredients except nutmeg together in a blender, or combine in a cocktail shaker and shake until frothy.

Pour into punch glasses, sprinkle nutmeg on top, and serve.

Serves 6.

Black Beans and Rum with Rice
Lolis Eric Elie
Cookbook author and TV producer/writer

Cookbook author Lolis Eric Elie was born and raised in New Orleans. He is a cofounder of the Southern Foodways Alliance. Working with director Dawn Logsdon, he co-produced the PBS documentary "Faubourg Tremé: The Untold Story of Black New Orleans." For three years, he served as a writer for HBO's "Treme" and is a writer for the AMC show "Hell on Wheels."

He first tasted Austin Leslie's version of this dish at Creole Feast, the festival created in 1978 by civil-rights activist and cookbook author Rudy Lombard to celebrate our indigenous food. While a pot of red beans and rice has long been a staple at parade parties, here is Elie's twist on it, inspired by one of New Orleans' most revered chefs: "This is a recipe inspired by the late Austin Leslie. He made black beans with rum. I never got his recipe but invented my own. I serve it whenever I have a Carnival party in part as a nod to our fellow Gulf of Mexicans, the Cubans."

Lolis Eric Elie with his sister Migel Elizabeth Elie. (Courtesy of Lolis Eric Elie)

1 lb. dried black beans, rinsed and picked over
1 large onion, chopped
2 ribs celery, chopped
1 medium green bell pepper, chopped
4 tbsp. chopped fresh garlic
One 4-oz. jar sliced pimentos, not drained
3 large bay leaves
1 tbsp. Italian seasoning
½ cup olive oil
11 cups water
2 tsp. salt or to taste
1½ tsp. habanero pepper sauce or other hot sauce
4 tbsp. butter
½ cup dark rum
Cooked rice

In a heavy 6-qt. saucepan or large Dutch oven, combine the beans, onions, celery, bell pepper, garlic, pimentos and their juice, bay leaves, Italian seasoning, olive oil, and water. Bring to a boil over high heat. Reduce the heat to medium low, cover the pan, and cook until done, about 3 hours, stirring about every 15 minutes to prevent the beans from sticking to the bottom. The finished beans should be tender and most of them still whole, all sitting in a thick bean jus.

Add the salt, then the hot sauce, then the butter, then the rum. Continue cooking for 10 minutes more. Serve with rice.

Serves 5-6.

The Original "BB" King Cake
Chef David Guas
Owner of Bayou Bakery, Coffee Bar & Eatery in Arlington, Virginia

Chef David Guas was born in New Orleans. (Photo by Scott Suchman)

Following a thirteen-year pastry-chef career, New Orleans-born chef David Guas is now the owner of Bayou Bakery, Coffee Bar & Eatery in Arlington, Virginia. He is also the author of the critically acclaimed cookbook *DamGoodSweet: Desserts to Satisfy Your Sweet Tooth New Orleans Style*. Guas makes frequent appearances on NBC's "Today." He was a finalist for *Food & Wine*'s People's Best New Chef in the Country for 2011 and 2012 and has appeared on Food Network's "Chopped" and the Cooking Channel's "Unique Sweets." Guas has also been featured in *Cooking Light, Food Arts, Chocolatier, Pastry Arts & Design, Esquire, Men's Health Magazine, New York Times*, and *Garden & Gun Magazine*.

KING CAKE
1 pkg. (¼ oz.) dry-active yeast
¼ cup milk, warmed (105-115 degrees or warm to the touch)
1 cup plus 6 tbsp. bread flour (plus extra for rolling)
1 tbsp. honey

A slice of Original "BB" King Cake with cream-cheese filling, created by Chef David Guas. (Courtesy of Bayou Bakery, Coffee Bar & Eatery)

¾ cup cake flour
2 large eggs
1 large egg yolk
2 tbsp. sugar
½ tsp. ground cinnamon
½ tsp. vanilla extract
¼ tsp. almond extract
1 tsp. salt
5 tbsp. unsalted butter, room temperature
1 plastic baby figurine (to hide in the cake), optional

Whisk the yeast with the warm milk in the bowl of a stand mixer until dissolved. Add the 6 tbsp. bread flour and the honey and, using the paddle attachment, mix on low speed until fairly smooth (there will still be a few lumps), 30 seconds to 1 minute, scraping the bottom and sides of the bowl as necessary. Cover with plastic wrap and let rise until doubled in volume, about 20 minutes.

Once the dough has doubled, add ¾ cup of the remaining bread flour, the cake flour, eggs, egg yolk, sugar, cinnamon, vanilla and almond extracts, and salt. Mix on low speed until combined, then switch to a dough hook, increase the speed to medium, and beat until smooth, about 2 minutes. Increase the speed to medium high and begin adding 4 tbsp. of the butter 1 tbsp. at a time, mixing well between additions.

Continue to knead until the dough forms a slack ball (it will ride the dough hook, be tacky, and not slap the bottom of the bowl, but it should generally come together into a loose mass), 2 to 3 minutes. If the dough doesn't come together, continue kneading while adding up to ¼ cup of the reserved bread flour, until it does.

Grease a large bowl with ½ tbsp. of the remaining butter and transfer the dough to the bowl, turning it over in the bowl to coat with butter. Cover the bowl with plastic wrap or a damp kitchen towel and place in a draft-free spot until the dough has doubled in size, about 1 hour.

Line a rimmed baking sheet with parchment paper and grease the parchment paper with the remaining butter. Generously flour your work surface using the remaining ¼ cup bread flour (if you used the bread flour in the dough, dust your work surface with more bread flour). Turn the dough out onto the work surface and sprinkle the top with some flour. Use your hands to press and flatten the dough into a rectangle. Using a rolling pin, roll the dough into a ½–in.-thick strip that is about 24 in. long by about 6 in. wide.

CINNAMON SUGAR
¼ cup sugar
2 tsp. ground cinnamon

CREAM CHEESE FILLING
2½ tbsp. cornstarch
¼ cup sugar
9 oz. cream cheese, softened
¼ tsp. vanilla extract
¼ tsp. lemon extract
1 egg

Mix cinnamon and sugar, and sprinkle on dough strip.

For filling, combine cornstarch with sugar in a bowl. Place the cream cheese in the bowl of a mixer and, using the paddle attachment, beat for 1 minute. Add the sugar mixture and beat on medium high until smooth, scraping down the sides of the bowl. Slowly add extracts with egg until smooth.

Using a pastry bag with a plain, round tip, pipe a straight, ¼-in.-thick line of the filling down the dough strip, spaced 1 in. from the edge. Starting with that edge, roll the dough over the filling, and continue to roll the dough all the way up, like a jellyroll. Pinch the edge to the body of the dough to seal, turn the dough so it lies horizontally on your work surface, and gently roll it on your work surface to even out any bulges and create a somewhat consistent 1½–in.-wide rope.

Bring the two ends of the dough together, making an oval or circle, and pinch the ends into one another to seal. Carefully transfer the dough oval or circle to the prepared baking sheet. Cover with plastic wrap or a damp kitchen towel and set in a warm, dry spot to rise until doubled, about 1 hour.

EGG WASH
1 large egg
1 tbsp. milk

Heat the oven to 375 degrees. To make the egg wash, whisk the egg and milk together in a small bowl. Brush the egg wash over the top and sides of the dough, and bake the king cake until golden and cooked through, 25 to 30 minutes. Immediately after removing the cake from the oven, make a small slit in the bottom of the cake and insert the baby figurine (if using). Set cake on a rack to cool completely.

ICING AND DECORATION
2 cups powdered sugar, sifted
2 tbsp. light corn syrup
3 tbsp. milk
¼ tsp. vanilla extract
3 cups sugar
Green food coloring
Gold or yellow food coloring
Purple or red and blue food coloring

While the cake cools, make the icing. Whisk the powdered sugar, corn syrup, milk, and vanilla together in the bowl of a stand mixer on low speed until smooth and completely incorporated. Cover the bowl with a damp kitchen towel until you are ready to glaze the cake.

To make the colored sugar, measure 1 cup of the sugar into each of 3 zip-type, quart-size plastic bags. Add 4 drops green food coloring to one bag, 4 drops gold or yellow food coloring to another bag, and 4 drops purple food coloring to the last bag (if you don't have purple, make it yourself: measure 2 drops red and 2 drops blue food coloring onto a spoon and mix with a cake tester or toothpick until combined). Seal each bag and then vigorously shake to combine the sugar and food coloring.

Spoon the icing over the cooled cake. Immediately after icing, decorate with the tinted sugar. I like to alternate colors every 2½ in., but you can also apply one color to each of 3 equal sections. Slice and serve immediately, or store in a cake box or on a baking sheet placed within a large plastic bag (unscented trash bags work well) for up to 2 days.

Serves 12-14.

Ash Wednesday

Ash Wednesday resonates in New Orleans more than in most places because of the way we live the day before. There would be less purpose in saying "farewell to flesh" were we not previously so consumed by flesh of all forms. The simplicity of ash smudges on foreheads is a counterpoint to vividly painted faces.

On Ash Wednesday morning in the French Quarter, merchants sweep their sidewalks. Where on the day before the air was permeated with the smell of fast food, the smell the morning after is of pine oil chasing stains. Beads, which for the previous two weeks had been flying through the air, bouncing off buildings, and crash landing on trees as revelers leaped to snag them, are now humbled on Ash Wednesday, coiled in the gutter, awaiting the man with the broom and shovel. A few escaped doubloons and blinky items, having lost their flicker, join the pile.

Necks, which on the previous day were piled high with those beads, are now adorned with just a simple tie, necklace, or open collar. Suddenly we have landed in the middle of the work week. Reality sets in. City busses now travel what was the path of kings in the days before. Commerce returns to where abandonment reigned.

We're told to fast on the day after Mardi Gras, though there is still leftover party food. Yet there is relief in being spared more MoonPie* with champagne. By Ash Wednesday, simplicity is welcomed. It is the tonic we need, so that one day we can return to the flesh and then say farewell again.

Mardi Gras Day on Royal Street in the French Quarter. (Photo © Judi Bottoni)

As the celebration winds down, a group of New Orleans policemen traditionally rides down Bourbon Street on horseback to let revelers know that it's time to go home. (Photo © Mitchel Osborne)

Opposite: *These Krewe of Babylon lieutenants allow some tiny parade-goers a peek behind their masks.* (Photo © Mitchel Osborne)

This rare photo shows the Jefferson City Buzzards marching club about to embark on their route through Uptown New Orleans in 1900. Founded in 1890, they continue to march on Mardi Gras and a few other times during the year. (Courtesy of Richard Hofler and the Jefferson City Buzzards)

Opposite: *From an 1858 edition of the French publication* Illustration, Journal Universal, *depicting Ash Wednesday, the first day of Lent.* (From the collection of Peggy Scott Laborde)

This reveler reminds us that almost everywhere else in the world, Mardi Gras Day is just a regular day. (Photo by Peggy Scott Laborde)

The author would like to acknowledge the generous assistance of The Historic New Orleans Collection in providing some of the images contained in this book.

THE COLLECTION

THE HISTORIC NEW ORLEANS COLLECTION

533 Royal Street • 70130-2179 • www.hnoc.org • (504) 523-4662

The Historic New Orleans Collection, founded in 1966, is a museum, research center, and publisher located in the heart of the French Quarter. Founders L. Kemper and Leila Williams were avid preservationists and collectors of manuscript materials relating to the Battle of New Orleans and French colonial society. Over time, THNOC's collecting mission has expanded to include photography, film, jazz, literature, decorative arts, costumes, and oral history narratives. Researchers may access the institution's holdings, which include more than thirty-five thousand library items, at the Williams Research Center, one of the largest archives in the South.

In THNOC's galleries, the museum presents changing exhibitions on topics related to the history and culture of New Orleans, Louisiana, and the Gulf South. Guided tours of the galleries and grounds are led by trained docents. The programming schedule, always active, has become even more vibrant since Hurricane Katrina, an event that reminded all of us—on staff, and in the community—of the importance of preserving and celebrating the region's culture. Programming highlights include an annual research symposium in January, an annual antiques forum in August, monthly concerts, and targeted lectures and colloquia at regular intervals throughout the year.

Index